STONE MOVERS

ON MISSION WITH JESUS

Pastor Paul Sandberg

STONE MOVERS
Pastor Paul Sandberg

Copyright © 2019 by Pastor Paul Sandberg

Stone Movers International
1 Eldorado Drive, East Northport, New York, 11731

Bold portions of Scripture quotations and the italics are the emphasis of the author.

Illustrations by Rose C. Miller

Editors: Fran Fernandez, Lory Moses, Dale Moses, Tom Tengelsen, John DeMarco

ISBN-10: 9781096222026

CONTENTS

Introduction

I have sometimes thought about God letting me design my own life. If He had given me a pad of paper and told me to write anything I wanted and He would just follow my plan, what would have happened? Well, first I would have eliminated all conflict. Then I would have done away with most every kind of work. I would have designed a "perfect " life for myself.

One thing is for sure: I would never have had the guts or insight to write a life story that has been as exciting as my life has been! When I look back on my life I wonder how I made it through some of those serious situations. However, I HAVE been given a perfect life! Not a life full of ease and entertainment, but a life full of adventure! I have come to learn that a perfect life is not a trouble free life. A perfect life is full of trouble and conflict, but within that life is the awesome presence of our Lord. In a perfect life, the Lord Jesus supplies the strength, insight, and grace to weather the storms, endure the crisis, solve the problem, overcome the obstacle, and accept the things that are beyond our control. A perfect life sees and experiences the mercy, grace and glory of Jesus as He invites us into His presence.

Being a Christian has been the most exciting thing in my life. Being a pastor has been the most difficult thing I have ever done. But being a pastor has also been the most fulfilling thing I could ever imagine. The perfect life of my own design would have been boring and empty.

This book is a look at life in the realm of missions. It is focused largely on short-term trips and long-term commitments. This includes a look at some difficulties and troubles related to mission work, but also highlights the victories and the plan of the Lord to use each of us for His glorious purposes. The stories contained in these pages are real stories. Many of the names have been changed, but each story is real and true, not embellished or exaggerated.

Being used by the Lord to touch lives and communities with the Gospel is a privilege and honor. It is often breathtaking and inspiring when God chooses to use US. He works through us in people's lives to effect ETERNAL transformation in them. We cannot separate ourselves from the stories of what God is doing all around us. We are part of the story! So as you read through STONE MOVERS, please keep in mind that any and all victories, good decisions, insights, successes and changed lives are a result of God's grace and mercy. I count it an undeserved blessing to be part of the story.

My hope is that as you read STONE MOVERS, the Lord will give you insight, clarity, vision and motivation to begin or to continue serving in the area of missions.

Pastor Paul Sandberg

Chapter One
Stone Movers
John 11

Have you ever had a problem? I know you have. Everyone has problems. We are going to look at someone in the Bible who had a problem. A real problem. A serious problem. Actually, the most serious problem a person can have. His name was Lazarus, and he was dead! He was really very dead. There was no question about it. Not "Mostly Dead", but totally, completely and thoroughly dead. There is no greater problem a man can have. Lazarus was DEAD!

But let us begin to look at this problem a few days earlier in this course of events. We get this account from the Gospel of John, chapter eleven. Lazarus was very sick so Martha and Mary notified Jesus of the serious nature of his illness. Jesus loved Lazarus as well as Martha and Mary. As a result there were some expectations of what Jesus should do. Close friends and relatives were expected to respond immediately to the desperate needs of their loved ones, much like today.

I was in Cuba back when there was virtually no communication possible between that Island and the United States. While I was there my Mother became seriously ill and it was discovered that she was full of cancer. Somehow my wife got word to a pastor friend of mine in another part of Cuba, who tracked me down through some mutual friends nearby, and they sent a young boy on a bicycle out to the remote area where I was staying. The note just said, "Call your wife." I proceeded to the only phone in that little town, located in the front room of an old widow living on the main street, and spent 2 hours trying to get an international operator, and finally got to speak with my wife. When I was told the serious situation with my mother, I immediately made my way to the airport to try to get a flight home. Luckily I had grabbed my wallet, ID and Passport before heading out to the remote location days earlier. As I spoke to the agent at the airport I was told there was a flight leaving in 30 minutes, but I would need to travel through Montreal, Canada. I would need to spend the night there and catch a flight to New York in the morning. I paid the fare and jumped on the plane, only to realize that I was traveling to Montreal, Canada in February, where the average temperature was probably about 0 degrees, and I was wearing a tee shirt and sandals. No problem, I thought. I will just purchase socks and a sweatshirt in the Montreal Airport. Nope! Every store was closed because we landed after 10:00 pm. Also, every store in town was closed. No Shopping was going to happen. I was cold but I made it through the night in a hotel room and arrived in New York the next day. I got to my Mom's bedside and helped arrange for hospice care. Mom passed away a few weeks later.

What I did was not special; it was an automatic response to a serious situation. Isn't that what we do? We run to the side of the ones we love when crisis hits. We drop everything and react with urgency in an attempt to ease the pain of those we care about. Not Jesus. When he gets the word that Lazarus is very sick and needs Him, Jesus waits several days. He tells his followers "This sickness will not end in death." So there is an expectation that Jesus will heal Lazarus from whatever affliction is ailing him. That is no real surprise. It is certain that the followers of Jesus remember the Centurion Soldier who came to Jesus asking Him to heal his servant who was paralyzed and in great agony. The Gospel of Matthew, chapter 8, tells us that Jesus was willing to travel to the Centurion's home to heal the servant but the Centurion objected on the grounds that he was not worthy to have Jesus come under his roof. So Jesus healed the servant from a distance. The power of Jesus to heal is not constrained by location or distance. So the followers of Jesus knew full well that He could heal Lazarus from anywhere if He chose to do so. No Problem! Except Lazarus died! Then Jesus actually says, "Lazarus is dead!" There is no question, no mistake, and no doubt. Lazarus is dead, but Jesus told them earlier that this sickness would not end in death! This is very confusing to all those concerned.

Jesus finally decides to go to Lazarus. We do not know how long it took for Jesus to get to the town where Martha and Mary had lived with Lazarus, but we do know from John 11 that when Jesus arrived at the town Lazarus had been dead four days. Lazarus was not just a little dead or newly dead, he was very dead. He had been anointed with burial oils, wrapped in burial cloth, and placed in a tomb. His body had begun to decompose. (v39). Jesus walked into this situation and I believe the people, including Mary and Martha, were angry with Jesus. They had the expectation that Jesus would heal the one He loved, and that He would have hurried to the bedside of Lazarus to keep him alive. Or at the very least, heal Lazarus from a distance. After all, the Great Healer had publically stated that the sickness of Lazarus would not end in death, but it DID! Had Jesus lied to them? And both Martha and Mary accused Jesus of allowing the sickness of their brother to culminate in the agony of death when they said, "If you had been here our brother would not have died." The anger and disappointment are evident if we are able to put ourselves in the place of the family. They knew Jesus, His power, His ability, and His love for Lazarus, and their greatest expectations of Him were left unfulfilled. Even the crowd said in ridicule of Jesus, "Could He not have kept Lazarus alive?"

Then Jesus wept. This is somewhat puzzling. Jesus is in the middle of a crowd of family and friends mourning the death of someone they all loved. There is great pain. And they are all mad at Jesus for letting this happen. However, Jesus knows something that no one else is even remotely considering. Jesus knows that in just a few minutes Lazarus will be alive once again! Jesus is planning to raise Lazarus from the dead and change all of the mourning, pain and sadness into rejoicing! A mere man in this situation would be snickering, thinking to himself "Wait till they see what I am about to do! They are mad at me now, but in a few minutes I will be their hero. This is going to be awesome!" But Jesus is no mere man. He is Jesus, the Christ, the Savior and Lord of all. So Jesus wept!

I believe that as Jesus looked around He saw all the pain and sorrow and misery this death had caused. Since Jesus is God, I believe He also saw all of the pain and all of the sorrow and all of the misery that sin and death brought into the world for all of the past, present and future generations. So Jesus wept. Man was never created for pain; he was created to have a loving relationship with the Lord. But sin had destroyed that relationship. So Jesus wept.

Then Jesus walks over to the tomb where Lazarus is buried. Jesus, the creator of everything, stands before the tomb of a very dead man. Let us remember just who this Jesus actually is!

"All things were made through him, and without him was not anything made that was made." (John 1:3 ESV)

Jesus is God, Creator, and Lord of all.

Colossians 1:16-17 tells us that Jesus created all things, in heaven and on earth, and that through Jesus, all things hold together.

10

Jesus, the one who fed 5000 men with five loaves and two fish. Jesus, the one who walked on water, calmed the storm, the wind and the waves. Jesus, the one with power over ALL creation, stands in front of the tomb of a very dead man, and is about to defy death itself and solve the biggest problem a man can have by raising him from the dead. And the Lord Jesus says something very strange:

"Move the Stone."

Did Jesus need help? Did he forget He was God? Why didn't He just wave his hand and move the stone himself, or flick His wrist and toss the stone all the way into the Red Sea? He could have made the stone disappear, or explode in a brilliant exhibition of creative theatrics to set the stage for this amazing miracle that was about to take place. But no. Jesus just says,

"Move the Stone."

What is happening? What is Jesus doing? Let us think through this together. There are four aspects of this simple statement of Jesus we will look at, and four observations to apply. First the four aspects of the Miracle;

1) Lazarus is dead.

Lazarus is not able to move the stone himself. What was Jesus supposed to say? "Lazarus, do you want to be raised from the dead? If so, move the stone!" Lazarus is not able to respond to Jesus. He is dead. Jesus told the ten lepers (Luke 17) to go show themselves to the High Priest—and they were healed. Jesus told the man with the withered hand (Mark 3) to stretch it forth—and he was healed. Lazarus has no such ability. Death has rendered him incapable of helping his own situation in any way. Lazarus can do nothing.

2) Others COULD move the stone.

Moving the stone was well within the ability of the followers of Jesus. As a matter of fact, moving the stone was the ONLY thing they could do. They had tried to keep Lazarus from dying, and that was beyond their ability. And they had absolutely no hope of performing a miracle that would raise Lazarus from the dead. However, they could move the stone. The followers of Jesus had the ability to remove the obstacle that was standing between Jesus and Lazarus. They had the opportunity to do the ONLY thing they could do, move the stone, so that Jesus could do what ONLY He can do, raise Lazarus from the dead.

3) Jesus chooses.

Jesus chooses to use His followers as part of this great miracle. Jesus looked around and was determined to include those standing with Him in the victory He was about to have over death. He was not going to do this alone. Jesus was planning to raise Lazarus from the dead, but He was not going to do it until His followers acted in obedience and moved the stone. Jesus wanted to include His followers in this tremendous miracle, but He did not give His followers a detailed plan of what was about to happen. They just needed to have enough faith to be obedient. As a result of their obedience, they participated in this great miracle of victory over death. Who were these men? What were their names? The scripture does not tell us. No one will ever know who these men were. That is Awesome! Because Jesus gets all of the glory!

4) Friends and family could not.

Friends and family could not respond FOR Lazarus when Jesus said, "Lazarus, come out!" They could not run into the tomb and pick up Lazarus, drag his body out and prop it up under a tree and claim a resurrection! That would just be a dead guy leaning against a tree. There is no way to fake this. Somehow, the body of Lazarus must obey the command of Jesus and come out of the tomb. Lazarus himself must respond to Jesus on his own, no one can respond for him or in his place. No matter how holy they are and how hard they try, Mary and Martha cannot accept the new life that Jesus is offering to Lazarus. Only Lazarus has the power to receive new life from Jesus. How did a dead man respond to Jesus? That is the Miracle!

Now the four observations to apply;

1) Look around.

The world is full of dead people. Yes, they are walking around in bodies that contain physical life. But inside the souls of these people they are just as dead as Lazarus. They have a serious problem. Actually, the most serious problem a person can have. They are spiritually dead! They are very dead. There is no question about it. Not "Mostly Dead", but totally, completely and thoroughly dead. There is no greater problem. They are lost forever. They cannot see Jesus, much less know Him and have faith in Him. There is a big stone standing between them and Jesus. They are dead, they can't move the stone, and they don't even realize it is there. There is nothing they can do about it.

"For all have sinned and fall short of the glory of God."
(Romans 3:23 ESV)

"The LORD looks down from heaven on the children of man, to see if there are any who understand, who seek God. They have all turned aside; together they have become corrupt; there is none who does good, not even one." (Psalm 14:2-3 ESV)

2) The Followers of Jesus have a job.

The best thing the followers of Jesus can do to reach the spiritually dead is to remove the obstacle that is standing between them and Jesus. Actually, it is the ONLY thing His followers can do. The miracle of salvation and eternal life is far beyond their ability and control. But they can move the stone and clear the way so there is nothing blocking the way to keep the lost from seeing Jesus. What does that stone look like? It may be a broken relationship, or a forgiveness issue. Possibly the person has never met an authentic Christian, or maybe they have been hurt by someone professing to be a Christian. The society we live in is very loud and busy, and it is drifting more and more into self-indulgence. People can insulate themselves from their dead spiritual condition as they devote themselves to their own successes, careers and positions of power. They hide in their homes, turn up the music in their cars, lock themselves in their bedrooms, overeat, over exercise, over spend, and over react. These things are all stones that block people from contact with Jesus the Savior. Jesus is waiting to call them to eternal life.

"Do not love the world or anything in the world. If anyone loves the world, the love of the Father is not in him. For everything in the world—the cravings of sinful man, the lust of his eyes and the boasting of what he has and does—comes not from the Father but from the world."
(1 John 2:15-16 NIV)

3) Jesus chooses.

Jesus chooses to include His followers in His victory over Satan. The Gospel will be preached to every Tribe and Nation, every far away land, every corner of the earth, and every near and distant place. Jesus has a plan to reach your community, your workplace, your school, and your next-door neighbor with the miracle of rebirth, but He is not going to do it without you! The Lord has decided to use His friends to bring the miracle of Eternal Life to the spiritually dead. Jesus will do what ONLY he can do, raise the dead, when His obedient followers do the ONLY thing they can do, Move the Stones. And if we have the faith to be obedient, when we are gone from this earth, no one will remember our name, but lives will be changed and Jesus will get all the glory. All of the fruit of the harvest belongs to the Lord Jesus. It is His to share with us as He chooses.

"I no longer call you servants, because a servant does not know his master's business. Instead I have called you friends, for everything that I learned from my Father I have made known to you. You did not choose me, but I chose you and appointed you to go and bear fruit—fruit that will last." (John 15:15-16 NIV)

4) The Response.

The lost and the dead must respond to the call of Jesus for themselves. No pious parents can drag their unbelieving children into eternal life. No loving child can claim salvation for the parent they so dearly love. No dedicated wife can earn redemption for her husband, and no pastor can bestow rebirth upon any of his congregants. The miracle of the saving blood of our Lord is effective for each and every person as they individually respond to the call of Jesus. The response to the call to walk out of the tomb must me made by the one being called. There is no way to fake this. No parent, child, relative, spouse, or friend is able to respond in the place of another. We can only Move the Stone that stands between the person and Jesus, so there is no hindrance to the miracle Jesus desires to do.

"Truly, truly, I say to you, whoever hears my word and believes him who sent me has eternal life. He does not come into judgment, but has passed from death to life."
(John 5:24 ESV)

A Number of years ago I was planning to travel to Cuba. I was scheduled to fly out of the country at 9:00 pm that night, and I was not yet packed or ready to go! I would need to leave by 6:00 pm to get to the airport in time for my flight. It was noon. That's when the phone rang.

It was a woman in my church named Peggy. Her Mother was in the hospital near death. The entire family including her brothers, sisters and the cousins, were all planning to meet at the Hospital at 4:00 pm that afternoon to spend some time with their sickly Matriarch before she passed away. Peggy's Mom, Mary, was in a coma and had been non-responsive for the past two weeks. Time was short. Peggy wanted me to join the family at the hospital to lead them in prayer at 4:00 pm. "Could you please? It would mean so much to us!" Peggy pleaded. Mom is not a Christian and we need to pray for her! She is LOST!" I could hear the genuine concern in her voice. Peggy was the only Christian in her family. The thought of her Mom passing away without knowing Jesus was just too much for Peggy to accept. So she pleaded with me.

My brain was racing with thoughts; I had a flight to catch—to CUBA! I am leading a team on a mission trip to CUBA today! I am the Pastor! I need to pack, put some teachings together, and tie-up a million loose ends! She is asking too much! Is she crazy? There are other pastors on the church staff! But Peggy called ME!

I felt like Nehemiah when the King asked him "Why is your face sad?" Nehemiah had no time to begin a regiment of fasting and prayer. He had to answer the

King NOW! This could be a capitol offense! The King could have him put to death for having a sad face in his presence. Nehemiah just prayed in his heart "God help me"! Then he gave the King his answer. Likewise, while Peggy was pleading on the phone with me to go to the Hospital, and while my schedule of events flashed before my eyes, I prayed, "God, What should I do?"

I told Peggy I would meet the family at 4:00 pm for prayer in the hospital room.

I sort of finished my preparations for the trip at about 3:30 and made my way up to the hospital—getting to the room at just after 4:00 pm. The family was not there yet. I waited a few minutes. Mary was lying motionless in the bed. She was in a coma and completely non-responsive as Peggy had described to me.

At 4:15 I walked around a little. At 4:30 I checked the name on the door. At 4:45 I checked the name on the door again. This was at a time before cell phones and I didn't have Peggy's home phone number with me. At 5:00 pm I thought maybe I missed them! Did I have the correct time?

At 5:15 I decided to just pray for Peggy's Mom and leave. So I went over to the bed where Mary was lying quietly in a coma and I prayed a very nice prayer, touching her on the shoulder, holding her hand and asking her to squeeze my hand if she could hear me. I prayed and waited a moment. I received absolutely no response from her. What else could I do? So I turned to leave.

As I reached the door—I just could not leave! I cannot explain it, but I knew my job was not done. I walked back over to the bed and stood there. God then spoke to me. Sometimes I wish the Lord would just call

17

me on the phone and tell me what He wants me to do! I know he has my number! Then I would just do what He tells me. But no, I have never heard audible words from God. But God spoke to my heart, not audibly but very clearly He communicated His instructions to me. I felt "Pray with Mary as if you are Mary!" What? "Pray with Mary as if I am Mary?" I never did that before! How do I do it? I felt very awkward! Was I hearing correctly? I didn't feel free to leave that room until I "Prayed as if I was Mary!"

So I looked around the room to make sure no one was watching or listening. I looked down the hall to see if anyone was around. I was certainly alone with Mary. I bent over close to Mary's ear. I held her hand and spoke slowly and clearly. I introduced myself as Pastor Paul, and I told her "Mary, I am going to pray as if I am you. You do not need to say anything, you just need to agree with my prayers in your heart."

I looked around the room again to make sure I was alone, and began to pray, "Hello Lord, this is Mary. You know me, I'm Peggy's Mom." And I prayed a prayer as if I was Mary, thanking God for my family, the blessings I received throughout life, I thanked God for everything I knew about Mary and her family. Then I prayed a prayer of repentance for all of the sins I had committed. It must have sounded interesting to anyone who might have been listening to this prayer! I repented of everything the Lord brought to my mind and named a bunch of sins I was sorry I had committed. I then prayed a prayer of salvation. "Lord, this is Mary, and I am asking you to come live within my heart, I give my heart and my life to you, take away my sins and cleanse my soul with your precious blood." I prayed for quite a few minutes, then reminded God again that I was Mary, Peggy's Mom, and then reminded Mary that she just needed to agree with the prayer and she would be saved. AMEN!

There is a feeling we sometimes get when someone sneaks into the room unnoticed and just stands there without making a sound. They just wait for you to finish doing whatever it is you are doing. They just wait for you to notice them standing there! Then you realize that they have been watching the whole thing! Usually you are doing something that is hard to explain, like "Praying as if you were Mary!" Without looking I felt that someone was in the room with Mary and me! I stood up, turned around, and saw no one! The room was quiet, the hall was empty, and no one was there. I was there alone, just Mary and me. I gave a sigh of relief.

I reached in my pocket to get one of my cards to leave for the family. I did not want them to be disappointed if they thought I did not show up—but I had no cards with me! I had no wallet, no pen, no paper, and nothing to leave a note. It was after 5:30 and I had a plane to catch! I quickly left. No one knew I had been there.

I made my flight, conducted a successful mission trip to Cuba, and returned two weeks later. I landed Sunday afternoon and got home about 5:00 pm. My wife had a message for me.

Mary had passed away three days earlier, and Peggy had called to let me know. Also she invited me to the funeral home. Was the family mad at me? Did they think I had not gone to the hospital? I just had a sinking feeling in my stomach that the family was disappointed in me. I was the one they called on to give them comfort in their time of grief, and it never happened. I tried to prepare an explanation for them that would not sound like I was blaming them for missing the time in the hospital room two weeks earlier. After all, they were the grief stricken family who needed comfort. So I began to mentally prepare myself to take the blame.

I purposely arrived at the funeral home 10 minutes before closing so I could escape quickly if needed. As I walked into the funeral home Peggy saw me and called me over to introduce me to her whole family. I thought "Oh No! This is not going to be good. A public chastisement!"

Peggy assembled everyone in a circle and boldly proclaimed to her family and friends "This is Pastor Paul. He is the one who visited Mom in the hospital and led her to Jesus. Mom gave her heart to Jesus with Pastor Paul! That is how we KNOW Mom is now in heaven with Jesus!"

What was she talking about? No one knew I was there! What happened? So I asked Peggy "What are you talking about?" So Peggy told me that on the day the family was planning to meet me at the hospital to pray with mom, they had been delayed and did not get to the hospital until about 7:00 pm. When the family walked into the hospital room, Peggy touched her Mom on the shoulder. Mary opened her eyes and said to them all "Pastor Paul was just here. He introduced me to Jesus and I repented of my sins. Jesus is so nice! I gave my heart to Him. I am going to go live with Him soon!" Mary then lay back down, went back into a coma, never woke up again, and passed away almost two weeks later.

I do not believe in "Magic Prayers," but I do believe in true repentance and the grace of God! Romans 10:9-10 tells us "Confess with your mouth...and believe in you heart...and you will be saved." I had the honor of being Mary's lips as she confessed her faith in Jesus, and by doing so she confirmed the belief in her heart. At the last minute, just as the thief on the cross next to Jesus did, Mary secured her place in Heaven.

I am always amazed at the mercy and faithfulness of the Lord. He asked me to Move a Stone. I did not understand or realize what was really happening in that hospital room that day. The only thing I could do was to be obedient. The stone I moved was words. Mary could not articulate her thoughts. She certainly could not form words. I have no way of knowing what little part of the prayer I prayed "as if I was Mary" was the key, or if everything I said was right on target. But during that prayer the Stone was Moved and Mary came face to face with Jesus. The Lord patiently waited until 5:30 pm one Friday evening to ask a pastor who was in a hurry to catch a plane, to stop for a moment do the ONLY thing he could do, Move a Stone with prayer. Jesus then did what ONLY Jesus could do, He granted eternal life.

Jesus was the one that entered that hospital room unnoticed two weeks earlier. It was His presence I had felt. He watched as a busy pastor prayed. It was in that room that Jesus revealed Himself to Mary, face to face. He took her anxiety, gave her peace, and bestowed upon her the gift of Salvation. It was in that room that the final battle in the war for Mary's soul was won. In that room the victory was sealed.

I thought I felt something!

"Behold, now is the favorable time; behold, now is the day of salvation." (2 Corinthians 6:2 ESV)

This is our job in missions; To Move the Stones that Jesus asks us to move. Jesus has already paid the price for all of our misdeeds; every sin we have committed, every act of selfishness, and every one of our hidden, secret and shameful acts has been purposely gathered together and placed upon the back

21

of Jesus. Jesus willfully took up the burden of the sinful corruption of the world, and purchased salvation, restoration, and eternal life for all who call on His name. The glory is not ours to bask in; the fruit is not ours to take. All the glory and all the fruit belong to Jesus. The gift of God to US is eternal life through Jesus Christ our Lord (Romans 6:23). What could be better than that? We get to share that gift with our neighbors, our co-workers, a woman in a coma, and a lost and hurting world all around us. EVERYONE needs Him!

That is a Mission

"All we like sheep have gone astray; we have turned— every one—to his own way; and the LORD has laid on him the iniquity of us all." (Isaiah 53:6 ESV)

I trust you will enjoy our journey together as we explore the world of short-term missions.

Chapter Two
The Load and the Burden

I was a student in seminary for 20 years. I thought I was just raising a family and earning a living, but there was a lot more going on than I was aware of. I spent those 20 years of my life on the job as a carpenter, not in a classroom. At the age of eighteen I began work as an unskilled laborer and went on to establish my own successful construction business. I left that business to become a pastor at the age of 38.

Those 20 years were valuable years of extensive seminary training that can only be received in the trenches with everyday people. Studying the complexities of human nature is essential to achieving any degree of success in a business as diverse as home improvements, and mandatory for any level of pastoral ministry. In most businesses, especially the field of home contracting, it is necessary to deal with a wide spectrum of people whose personalities range from "nice" to "unreasonable" and occasionally "extremely unreasonable." To complicate matters even further, sometimes a personality swing can happen in the same person instantaneously!

Jesus entered His public ministry only after He spent years as a carpenter. That was no accident. He worked with wood that needed to be cut and shaped, drilled and nailed, and sometimes hit with a hammer. Sometimes a big hammer. Then He moved on to work with people. People can be stubborn and messy. Sometimes we just want to hit them with a big spiritual hammer to force them to conform to the image of Christ! But the Lord does not work that way.

I became accustomed to the "unreasonable" side of human nature as well as appreciative of the "nice" side of people. The "nice" side was actually more prevalent but far less memorable than the "unreasonable" side. Generally, my customers became my friends, but not always. I have sometimes been caught off guard by an interesting phenomenon. This phenomenon usually manifested itself when we worked on a house belonging to someone who had lived there for an extended period of time. Perhaps they had raised their children in this house, or they grew up in this home themselves and had purchased it from their parents or grandparents. When it came time to renovate the house, or at least do some much needed repair work or updating, the "nice" would sometimes swing to "unreasonable" in an instant.

The first time I encountered this phenomenon was early in my business career. I had been contracted to replace the front window of an older cape home. The house had originally been built with two small windows in the living room. The homeowner had lived there for over 25 years and had raised 3 children in that home. They wanted to install one very large bay window in place of the existing two small windows. We needed to remove most of the front wall, temporarily support the second story, reframe the front wall with a new support header, and install the new large window.

This was a two-day job. I explained the process as best as I could to the husband, wife, and to their 24 year old son and his wife who all lived there together. Everyone was in agreement. When the day came to actually do the job we hung plastic sheets up to contain the mess to one room, supported the second floor and began to remove the front wall. As you can imagine we used big saws, hammers, crowbars, and other large tools to carefully and precisely take out what was to be removed. At this point the "nice" homeowners changed into "extremely unreasonable" homeowners accusing us of destroying their home! The woman was hyperventilating and the husband was screaming that we were destroying their lives! The son's wife even threatened to sue us! "My home will never be the same" was the cry of anguish and dismay. But we were too far along in the process to put things back.

I comforted the homeowners carefully for the two days of the job. When the entire project was complete the homeowners were extremely pleased with the results, but remained angry with me for "causing them so much pain and stress!" What had they expected? An effortless, no mess, quiet, stress free, major home improvement?

I have seen this same type of situation happen over and over again. When a contractor executes a plan that is precisely what the customer has asked for, there is sometimes a disconnect from reality. A homeowner may somehow expect major changes to happen in their beloved house without anything being disturbed or changed, no one being inconvenienced and no schedule being disturbed. The contractor suddenly becomes the "Bad Guy" for doing a good job and exactly what was asked of him.

So what did I do? After 20 years in construction, **I became a Pastor**!

Being a pastor has been the hardest thing I have ever done, but it is also the most exciting, and most fulfilling thing I have ever done. Don't misunderstand me...being the husband to my incredible wife Karen, being a father to my three extraordinary boys, father-in-law to my three wonderful daughters-in-law, and now a grandfather to 8 absolutely perfect grandchildren, has been the thrill ride of my life, but I am now talking about the realm of work, career and calling.

I must admit there have been days when I have had the desire to give up ministry and go back to building THINGS rather than building PEOPLE. Pastoring can be so very difficult, but the most exciting and fulfilling thing I have ever attempted—is pastoring! The physical things I have built will someday turn to dust, but the people I have built up in Christ will live for eternity in the presence of Almighty God. There is no contest, no comparison, and no giving up!

Because of my background I became the pastor on staff who would be summoned when someone needed help. You know the people I am referring to. These are the people who walk in off the street with some pressing need, an emergency situation, homeless, hungry, electricity shut off, no heat, and so on.

One day I was called on because someone had come into the front office desperate for gas money. I was busy with something so I asked for the person to wait a few minutes. Ten minutes later I walked to the front office to greet a young man about 20 years old named Billy. Billy proceeded to explain that he was desperate for $40 to put gas in his car. He just got paid and did not have enough gas in the car to get to the bank in town to cash his check. He was driving by the church and pulled in with the hope that we might be compassionate enough to bail him out of a tough spot.

In an effort to help Billy I asked him to endorse the back of his paycheck and I could cash it for him right away. He would then have all the money he needed to put gas in his car. He fumbled with his words and told me that he was actually on his way to his boss's house in a town about 30 miles away, where he must first pick up his paycheck and then come all the way back to cash his check in this town. At this point Billy was getting agitated and began to demand that we help him because we are Christians and we are supposed to help people!

So since we **WERE** in a Christian church, and Billy accused me of being a Christian, and he has clearly asked for help I took the opportunity to give him the best help he could ever receive. I explained the importance of faith in Jesus and explained the gospel message clearly and simply so that Billy had no misconception as to who Jesus Christ is and why He is important to salvation. Billy got even more demanding, dropping his $40 request down to $20. He then informed me that he left his mother out in the car to wait for him. He had now been in the church building for over 30 minutes. It was extremely warm that day so I said, "Let's go see your mom," and I walked him out of the office and down the stairs.

As we walked outside onto the hot parking lot we approached a woman sitting in the driver's seat of a car—that was RUNNING! It had been running for 30 minutes with the A/C on! Billy started to stutter and his face turned all red. I snuck a look in the car and saw the gas gauge on half full. Billy began to walk around to the other side of the car to get in the passenger seat. I realized that I would never see Billy or his mom again, so I pulled out a $10 from my wallet and Billy's eyes lit up.

Allow me to pause this story here for just a moment. I was having a flashback as I held that $10 bill out to Billy. It is true what they say—your life can flash before your eyes in an instant. In my case it was not my life—but an event from 10 years earlier.

Ten years earlier a man named Peter called and I was in no mood to speak with him. The only contact I had ever had with him was when he would call from time to time to plead his case and relate some compelling story of misfortune that would put the responsibility for some looming consequence squarely on my shoulders. He had never come to church, even though he promised he would come each time I had invited him. Helping those in need is one of the joys in life, and an effective ministry tool to share the Gospel with people. But Peter was one of those people who I resisted helping. Something about him made me feel very uneasy and cautious but I was not sure what it was. I was sure to hear about his latest crisis, which was always way too neatly packaged and nearly impossible to verify. I immediately prayed for guidance as I told the secretary to put the call through.

As I listened to Peter's saga I pulled out the notes I had written the last time we had spoken three months earlier. I began to see some subtle inconsistencies and some outright lies that made it clear that I was listening to a well-rehearsed story that had dramatically grown in scope and intensity since last time we spoke. I asked a few pointed questions to confirm my suspicions. His wife, the fire in their apartment and all of their possessions about to be lost for lack of storage fees, his wife's death in that terrible fire, his homeless children, were all lies. Three months ago he was not married, had no kids and no apartment!

With this revelation I took the opportunity to give Peter a clear Gospel presentation and an invitation to come to church and receive the only help he really needed, Jesus. As always he assured me that he would be there, this time with his (non-existent) children, but what he really needed was money NOW to survive. I simply said "I don't give money to con artists, what you need is Jesus". There was deafening silence for about 10 seconds, then an eerie laugh and Peter said "There is plenty of money out there just waiting for me to get, and

30

I know how to work the system. I know how to get money from churches!" **CLICK**

As I sat in my office with a quiet telephone in my hand, I was thankful for having uncovered a scam, but I was saddened by my inability to reach a lost soul for Christ. I felt that somehow churches were to blame for being such easy targets and enabling people such as Peter to avoid God by "**Working the System**".

How many times does God light a fire under someone in order to move him or her into a place of need where they will be forced to turn to Him, but then some well meaning Church or Christian rushes in and puts out the flames by meeting the need and solving the problem that might drive that person into the arms of God? Too many times, I'm sure.

A Scripture came to mind.

"Bear one another's burdens, and so fulfill the law of Christ". (Galatians 6:2 ESV)

Unfortunately that is where many stop reading.

We Americans love to ride in on our white horse to save the day in a blaze of glory and in the process we solve any and all problems that come our way. In our crusade of righteousness we enable people like Peter to become dependent and dysfunctional to the point that their lives are often destroyed. We actually train people by our generosity to be dependent on us and to expect a handout rather than to work their way out of a difficult solution.

I am proud to be a citizen of the United States. As a nation we have been the most giving and benevolent nation the world has ever seen. Our citizens are by far the most compassionate people in history, and I am privileged to be a part of that. However, that generosity has become a tool of destruction when it has been overdone.

For example, we have done a grave disservice to the Native American Indian. In a fit of remorse over past atrocities, the U.S. Government made virtually all Native Americans "wards of the state," receiving houses and monthly income simply because they are Native Americans. The grave consequences of alcoholism, drug abuse, crime and lack of education existing on their reservations can be directly traced back to the guilt offering that has made them dependent instead of independent and removed the initiative for self actualization. In our quest to assuage our guilt, we have inflicted serious injury.

Yes, we must carry each other's burdens, but the problem in our benevolent approach to helping people is that we do not read far enough in Galatians. The Scripture puts the command to carry each other's burdens in perspective. It gives balance to the command to help and care for one another.

Without balance—a helping ministry becomes lopsided, dysfunctional, and causes damage rather than supplying help. If we read further in Galatians 6, verse 5 says,

"For each will have to bear his own load"
(Galatians 6:5 ESV)

There is a big difference between a "**load**" and a "**burden**." That was the hidden problem that bothered me about Peter. His whole purpose was to get someone else to carry his load. The "**load**" is the normal, every day amount that each of us must carry to get through life.

Scripture describes the human condition:

"By the sweat of your face you shall eat bread, till you return to the ground." (Genesis 3:19 ESV)

"The desire of the sluggard kills him for his hands refuse to labor." (Prov. 21:25 ESV)

"If anyone is not willing to work, let him not eat."
(2 Thess.3:10 ESV)

The principle is firmly established in scripture. It is necessary for each man to shoulder the responsibility of his own upkeep. To carry another's load is unfair to him in the same sense that carrying an infant into adulthood without teaching him to walk is unfair to the child.

How can they learn?
How can they grow?
How can they mature?

On the contrary, the "**burden**" is the excess amount of life's troubles that must be shared from time to time. When situations arise that are over and above the normal "load" that each person is expected to carry through life, the burden is to be shared by others.

The burden is most often a temporary condition that is alleviated without any permanent intervention. This is most often a situation such as a job loss, serious sickness, injury, accident, natural disaster, and so on. In most cases the burden disappears when the new job is landed, health restored, accident repaired, home rebuilt, and the like. This burden is shared by others until the injured, sick or unemployed person is able to move past the crisis. Then they can once again shoulder the load of their own responsibilities.

When the temporary burden is prolonged past the appropriate cut off point and others carry the individual's normal load responsibilities, unhealthy dependencies are created. We actually hurt people by helping them too much. Understanding this concept has made it easier for me to turn away people such as Peter who are trying to turn their irresponsibility into my responsibility.

As I discover what load a person has and what their burdens are, the decisions for benevolent help are much clearer. (By the way, I often choose to help someone who is trying to manipulate me to carry his or her load. I will do that by choice for a short period of time in order to have an opportunity to reach them for Christ. That then becomes an act of love to reach a person in spite of their less than honorable intentions.)

The **"Load and the Burden"** is a cornerstone principle in really helping people.

******

Let's Take This to the Mission Field

I have been a Missions Pastor since 1994. This whole concept of the "Load and the Burden" changed the way I viewed missions work, and this Biblical principle became the cornerstone of my approach to missions. There are things in the mission field that I had never been able to understand, such as;

1) A church plant in Europe that existed for over 50 years and grew to 5 congregations, but continued to be completely dependent on money, preachers, leaders, and an authority structure from the United States.

2) Churches in Central America who would not even try to tend to the repair of their facilities because they could just wait for work teams

from the U.S. to come and do the work. One local church member said to the Pastor when asked to help with the repair "Why should I bother to fix the church building? If we wait long enough the North Americans will come down and fix it!"

3) Many indigenous pastors I met in Africa who had been supported by churches in the U.S. (some for over 30 years) had no plans to end that support. When the North American missionary stationed in the area retired from the field after 42 years of service, most of those churches just collapsed.

4) There are countless church plants throughout the world that have ceased to exist when the missionary pastor has left.

The list goes on and on. The process seems to have been; To plant churches throughout the world that are dependent and unable to exist without the missionary, or mission board, or the building that the mission board holds the title to, or money from supporters, or a worldview that says a real Christian church must be led by foreigners—because they have never had an indigenous Pastor.

What has happened?

In an effort to do what is right and good, great effort and resources have been poured into the carrying of the "**load**" of indigenous churches only to make dysfunctional cripples out of them.

A parent's objective should be to launch their children into the world as well adjusted, healthy adults, able to function and contribute to society. Likewise the church planter and missionary should launch their disciples into ministry as well adjusted, healthy leaders able to minister and evangelize on their own.

How do we do this?

We must look at the mission field with the eyes and focus of parents who are training their children to succeed. What is the "Load" that they must carry and what is the "Burden" that we must help them with? If we can determine these two things, the rest of the decisions will be much easier to make and stick to. Once we can determine the "Load" in the mission field that the indigenous people are able to perform well and take responsibility for, we can determine the "Burden" that weighs them down with responsibilities that they are unable to carry out, or ill equipped to handle.

This is an exciting dynamic to embrace because it enables us to form real, meaningful partnerships, solve real problems, and advance the Gospel of Jesus Christ by empowering and encouraging nationals to fulfill the calling of God on their lives to reach their own country for Christ.

The "us and them" mentality portrayed here will disappear as maturity and growth take place.

The healthy relationships we form will keep us from becoming legalistically rigid as we apply the Load and Burden concepts. It is certainly healthy to help a friend, neighbor or family member work on a project— even if they are more skilled than we are and don't really need our help. We do it out of friendship and support. Let me explain the balance needed.

My short-term team to Central America was once delayed from leaving to fly home to New York because of a massive snowstorm that blanketed the East Coast of the United States. While our families back home were getting snowed in, we were stuck for five extra days in 90-degree heat in Nicaragua! I spoke to the ministry director to see if we could be of assistance during the extra time we were there. They had several maintenance projects around the facility in progress, so we plugged in. We painted some buildings, dug some holes for a drainage system, and helped organize a large storage closet. These were all projects that fit squarely in the "Load" category of that local ministry. They had plenty of skilled workers on staff and they were very capable of completing the tasks without our help. However, we have had a great relationship with our friends in this ministry and we enjoy working with them. So we helped them with their "Load" of finishing these projects.

We were there in Nicaragua with five days to spare. Painting, cleaning and digging were certainly within the ability of the team. We were not going to sit around and watch them work, so we helped. It was healthy and it supported our already solid relationship.

No unhealthy dependencies were developed, and no unrealistic expectations were formed. We did not send a team to Central America to clean out a closet, or dig ditches, or paint. We did not take valuable work away from local workers; we just helped our friends while we were there. I am sure you see the difference.

Great care must be taken not to push the people who are being helped out of the way as help is being given to them. Pastors, missionaries, teachers, prayer teams, work teams, must all work **with** the people, **not in place of** or **in charge of** them. This goes against our built in North American "save the day" approach, which is fueled by the exciting prospect of being involved in forbidden lands and exotic places.

We have the golden opportunity to help birth healthy, interdependent churches, rather than dependent, crippled churches. We also need to balance our church planting approach without compromising the Gospel or by letting untrained and unprepared leadership steer people down the wrong road as we congratulate ourselves for making everyone feel good about themselves.

Long-term as well as short-term mission efforts have suffered greatly because very often this simple concept of distinguishing between the "**Load**" and the "**Burden**" has been overlooked.

The following chapters outline five non-negotiable aspects of short-term mission trips. These five areas also apply to long-term missions work with a few variations. If we incorporate this Biblical "Load and Burden" concept to our missions work internationally and locally, we will be much more effective as we help build the Kingdom of God worldwide.

But first let me get back to Billy. We were standing in the parking lot and I was holding a $10 bill in my hand. Billy's eyes were all lit up. I said "I will give you this $10 on one condition." He said "Sure". I told him "Don't agree to it until you understand the condition. Before I give you this $10 I want your permission to pray for you and your mom. I will pray that if you have been telling me the truth God will richly bless you, but if you have been lying to me God will discipline you. Alright?" Both Billy and his mom agreed so I put a hand on each of their shoulders and began to pray. "Lord, thank you that Billy and his mom found their way here on this day to seek help in their time of need. I pray that if they have been honest and truthful in their words that you will take this $10 and multiply it many times into a blessing too great for them to ignore and may they rejoice and give you all the glory and praise for meeting their need at this time. May you reveal yourself as the benevolent God and Father that you are. BUT, if they have lied about their need, or been deceitful about their intentions, will you please discipline them, PAINFULLY if needed! Do not let them escape, spare them death but bring them to repentance of their sin and a true and saving knowledge of Jesus, proving your love for them and granting them restoration for eternity. In Jesus name I pray. Amen"

As I lifted my head, Billy and his mom were wide eyed. Billy slowly reached out and took the $10 and just as slowly walked around the other side of the car. I quietly said to both of them "If you ever need to get out from under painful discipline, just come back here. My door is always open to you. We can set things right between you and God whenever you are ready. He is a God of restoration, not condemnation".

They pulled out of the parking lot and I was sad once again, having not been able to reach two lost souls for Christ. They could have chosen the vast riches of Salvation, Restoration and Eternal Life through knowing Jesus, but instead they chose to take $10. For years every Sunday I looked around to see if Billy and his mom might walk in. Maybe some day they will.

Construction is similar regardless of whether it takes place in someone's home or in someone's heart. People tend to expect their heart to be changed, rebuilt, renovated, purified or totally replaced without experiencing any inconvenience, mess, work, or pain. Even though it is God doing all the work, we must accept the process and do our part. God is a Gentleman; He will never force himself on anyone. He may reveal Himself in powerful and dynamic ways, but He will not force us to love Him. Sometimes we ask God to come into our lives and completely renovate us, make us new, make us into vessels of honor. We plead with Him to change us. Then when He begins His work in us, we become "extremely unreasonable!" We accuse Him of destroying our life as we cry in anguish and dismay. We even threaten Him. We get angry at Him for the pain we have caused ourselves in our own lives. The problem is that we insist on carrying a burden that is far beyond our ability to carry: Our **BURDEN** of Sin. We hold on to our sin and refuse to release it, yet we expect God to solve every little problem we have in life that is really our "**LOAD**".

Jesus took our hopeless burden of sin to the cross at Calvary, so we need to stop trying to carry it ourselves. We must release our lives to the Jewish Carpenter who promises to renovate and restore our lives. Scripture tells us,

"Therefore, if anyone is in Christ, he is a new creation. The old has passed away; behold, the new has come."
(2 Corinthians 5:17 ESV)

When the project of our sanctification is complete, we will be more than pleased with the results. Let us resolve not to resist God when He does exactly what we have asked Him to do in our lives.

In Missions, let us put away our own wants and desires, our quest for adventure and thirst for new and exciting experiences. Let us concentrate on what God wants to do through us.

I guarantee the Lord has a better and more exciting plan than you do!

I know it's not the best mission statement, but we can revise it after we figure out why we are going...

Chapter Three
There Must be A Reason

Non-Negotiable #1

While on the phone discussing a possible trip with some missionaries we work with in Europe I asked them "What needs do you have and how can I help you when I get there?" There was silence on the other end of the phone. Finally I heard "Well, I guess we need peanut butter." After another short pause they said "We've never been asked by someone how they can help us when they come over!" This leads us to the first "non-negotiable" of a short-term mission trip.

Non-Negotiable #1:
There Must be a Reason to Go.

When Jesus embarked on the greatest missionary journey in all eternity, He came to Earth for something specific.

He was not on vacation.

He was not shopping.

He was not looking for an adventure.

He came with purpose and focus. He had a **REASON** to come to Earth.

The reason the Son of God became man and dwelt among us was to bring Salvation to a lost and hopeless world.

Jesus was sent by His Father on a missionary journey to save mankind from the wages of sin. In the Gospel of John Jesus is recorded as saying,

"Peace be with you. As the Father has sent me, even so I am sending you." (John 20:21 ESV)

In many ways we have lost sight of the **REASON** Jesus has sent us out on mission. Instead of bringing peace, we bring frustration—for the team as well as the lost.

I was once asked by a missionary to visit him in Africa and bring a team of 10 people with me. This was a trip that at the time would cost about $4000 for each person and take three weeks.

When I asked what the team would be doing while in Africa the missionary said "Don't worry, we'll find something for them to do." The thought of spending $40,000 for ten people to travel to Africa to just "find something to do" did not seem wise to me, so I pressed harder for a reason to bring a team to Africa. I was told, "Well, you could paint the fence." This was a large piece of property that was all fenced in and would probably take ten people two weeks to paint, but why not just send $3000? That would cover the cost of purchasing the paint and hiring local laborers who desperately need the work?

Why should we spend an extra $37,000 to send people who don't know how to paint—to take away jobs from local skilled painters who desperately need the work?

Something is wrong with this.

This is not mission work; this is "make believe" mission work. All too often teams travel to exotic foreign lands on mission trips, or full time missionaries commit to extended periods of time in distant places, only to spend a lot of time, effort, money and resources accomplishing tasks that could be executed faster, cheaper, and with better results by local people.

These short and long-term missionaries then return to their home churches with great and wonderful stories of all the great things they have accomplished, the lives they have changed, and their own life changing experience.

They "**make believe**" that this is real mission work and that they have served a vital purpose in the preaching of the Gospel. All they have really done is spend a lot of money to take away employment from people who need the work, and accomplish tasks at a lower standard of quality than local craftsmen and laborers could supply.

Many foreign nationals dread the arrival of mission teams into their area to "help" because the teams take away valuable work from local people, and when the team leaves the work they did must sometimes be re-done because it is so shoddy.

This is also true of teaching, counseling and ministry teams that show up on the mission field with their newest favorite program to promote. They often convince themselves that their current specialty is exactly what is needed in the particular mission field they want to travel to. When the team leaves to go back home after spending long hours sharing the latest techniques and approaches to church growth and evangelism, or performing mimes and skits, the local pastors are often left with the task of repairing the damage of careless teaching and culturally inappropriate instruction.

Some teams have caused more damage than good.

There must be a viable need that this short-term mission trip will fill.

This is not a vacation with religious overtones. If someone wants a vacation they should take a vacation, not a mission trip. There are real needs and problems on the mission field and the short-term missionary must be focused on and prepared to meet needs and solve problems.

How is this done?

How do we discover the needs and problems in the mission field?

How do we solve real problems in a cross-cultural context?

Where do we begin?

The answers are surprisingly simple.

As I mentioned in the previous chapter, I became the Missions Pastor at my home church after I had spent 20 years in the construction field. For many of those years I owned my own company. We had a very successful business because we were able to solve problems for our customers.

The challenge was in discovering the real needs of a prospective customer and then making sure we both understood and agreed on those needs. Finally, designing a plan, project, or approach and meeting the need. At this point the prospective customer usually transitioned into a loyal client.

The process is surprisingly simple:

First, ask questions.
Second, find the real needs.
Third, design a solution.

This approach creates a successful relationship between the parties; each side benefits and problems are solved.

There are no pre-packaged solutions to people problems. For example; when I was giving an estimate for a kitchen renovation I would ask questions of the potential customer that would tell me what type of food they liked to cook, how much they liked to entertain guests, how many people were in the family and how many of them ate at home, what their favorite restaurant was, and what similar homes in the area had kitchen renovations that they liked.

I looked at their home closely and listened intently. I sometimes needed to design a kitchen to meet the food preparation needs of a large family in a workable design that was simple, neat, easy to clean, and within a strict budget **OR** I might need to come up with a design that was dramatic and an eye popping centerpiece to the house that would out shine the neighbors—and the budget was fully adjustable—and they never cooked at home anyway!

These are two very different sets of needs and the customer will most probably not explain those needs with words. Both sets of needs are real and valid, and if I wanted to land the job I must discover the **real** need and offer a **real** solution that solves their **real** problem.

The construction industry addresses people problems from a physical perspective, but the missionary, pastor, and ministry worker all approach people problems from a spiritual perspective.

Both the carpenter and the counselor are problem solvers.

Take this approach into short-term missions. Ask the missionaries, national leaders, and indigenous ministries what the problems are. You will need to listen real hard, and ask more questions. If you pay close attention sooner or later you will come to understand what the real issues are, and what kind of help is actually needed.

What are the things that they **CANNOT** do for themselves, and therefore need help with. They need help from someone who can come alongside and assist them as a brother.

This WILL take time.

You WILL make mistakes as you begin to help.

You may make several trips to the same location before the people there trust you enough to allow a glimpse of their real world to reach you.

Unfortunately, North American churches rarely take the time to do this today.

More often than not, a church develops a program, mime, singing group, marriage seminar, Bible training, teaching workshop, prayer team, church planter training, or something else that they are very excited about and are very good at. This church may have had wonderful results at home from this area of ministry and feel that they must share their success with the rest of the Christian world, and especially the mission field. They look around the world to find missionaries who will allow them to come and minister, and they take this program "On the road".

Some of these churches and organizations are very skilled at motivating their people to get involved. They put together large teams of talented people and they travel to a different part of the world every year. Sometimes they go to the same place two or three times in a row, and then change their focus to another part of the world. As a result of the changing destinations they never really discover the true needs of the people they are attempting to help. It is possible that the only real need being met is their own quest for adventure.

Or, some of these mission trips aren't really mission trips at all. They are actually:

Church events.

At remote locations.

That include service projects.

And have cross cultural elements included.

These can be AWESOME trips for the church congregation. People can grow in their faith, or even come to true faith for the first time. But are these really mission trips that answer the Biblical call to GO?

There are five commissions from Jesus in Scripture that instruct us to go and reach the world with the Gospel. There is one commission in each Gospel and one in Acts.

William L. Banks does a good job of covering these five in his book "In Search of the Great Commission" published by Moody Press. It is clear from these five commissions that mission teams have an important and distinct reason to GO; that reason is to teach, make disciples, and baptize people into faith in Jesus. The results are equally as clear; those who believe will be saved, those who do not believe are condemned. *(Matthew 28:18-20, Mark 16:15-16, Luke 24:46-47, John 20:21, and Acts 1:8.)*

This is serious business, and if we are serious about answering the call to GO, then we must be serious about the REASON we are going. We must ask ourselves "What are the needs we should be on the lookout for? What problems am I solving? What solutions can we offer? And how will this help spread the Gospel?"

There are **Five** different valid reasons for taking a short term mission trip. Let us explore them together and see how they lead us to fulfilling the Great Commission:

☐ **One - The Survey Trip.**

This may be the most important step in the process of setting up a mission trip.

A proper Survey trip will set you up for success in subsequent trips to that location and pave the way for a healthy relationship to form between the "Senders" and "Receivers." Before you commit your time, resources, energy and emotions, you should take a **SMALL** team (2-5 people) to the mission field you feel led to get involved with. If I lead a team from another church on a trip, I have already completed this step so they can have confidence in the fact that I am bringing them to a healthy place to minister and get involved. At the level that short-term teams plug into ministry—there needs to be some level of spiritual health and well-being already established on the field.

There are four main things to look for on a survey trip that will determine your involvement.

1) **Doctrine**.

Does the missionary, indigenous church, organization, and/or denomination you will be working with have solid doctrine? What do they believe? Are their main or core beliefs the same as yours?

Be flexible on the "Fringe" teachings, such as worship style, but do not compromise on the core beliefs such as; Jesus is God, Jesus is the only way of salvation, the Bible is the word of God, etc.

I visited a church in Africa that was asking for assistance and the **ONLY** topic the pastor would preach on was "prayer and fasting." I appreciate prayer and fasting, but when I asked about how he presented Jesus to the congregation he told me, "Jesus did His thing 2000 years ago! Now it all depends on prayer and fasting brother!" For that church Jesus was a fringe doctrine that was rarely if ever discussed. As a result we did not partner with that pastor or church, but we will be inviting him to future pastor training sessions!

As you help people in a foreign land achieve success reaching into the lost world within their communities—be aware of what teachings they are reaching into those communities with! If their doctrine is not sound, you probably do not have the time and resources to "straighten them out". **Remember, this is a short-term mission trip**, and we are talking about the missionaries or local church you will be partnering with. You will be working under their authority to advance the cause of the Gospel for the long-term.

You will just cause pain and problems if you try to change them. You need to work **WITH** them to reach out to their community where change is needed! Choose carefully the people and organizations that you partner with so you will be evenly yoked. Having said that, I have helped with pastoral training in countries where there was very little Biblical depth. More about that when we talk about teaching and training trips.

2) **Authority Structure**

Is there a healthy authority structure in place? Does the pastor you are seeking to help have anyone in country to hold him accountable? If there is a moral problem on this mission field, how is it handled?

I once stumbled upon a situation on the mission field that involved a Pastor who had a major moral collapse of a sexual nature. I became aware of it because those in authority above him had become friends of mine. They opened their "dirty laundry" and asked for my advice, even though they had a fear that once I was aware of the situation I might distance myself from them.

When I discovered how they had handled the situation I was very impressed with their commitment to Biblical principles. They had confronted the Pastor in question with the facts, and he acknowledged his actions but refused to stop. He was removed from ministry and put under church discipline according to the teachings of Jesus contained in Matthew 18. This was done at great cost to the denomination. Because of local laws the house-church he was pastoring was deeded in that pastor's name, so the denomination lost that house when they removed the pastor from ministry.

I was so impressed with the commitment of these leaders to not tolerate willful sin that I was encouraged to work with them MORE, not less. Their authority structure was Biblical and strong; they held each other accountable. We cannot supply that structure on a short-term trip, it must already exist on the mission field that we are assisting.

3) **Successes**.

What are they doing well? There must be some important areas where this local church or ministry is enjoying success. Find out about those areas.

> Is it their worship?
> Their community outreach?
> How they network together?
> Meet in each other's houses?
> Corporate prayer?
> Preaching?
> Bible studies?
> Ministry to children?
> Feeding program?

In what areas are they successful? Encourage them in these. Be careful not to crush their spirits by bringing in a team that will make them feel foolish because your team is so much more advanced. In fact you could probably bring in a team from your church or ministry in most ANY area of ministry and be superior to the local church in a third world country. Instead, once you have found out what they are doing well—encourage them and build them up in that area without competing with them. Then look for the fourth main thing.

4) **Problems**

You just discovered what they **ARE** doing well and you encouraged them. You are now in a position to discover the real reason for your mission trip. What are they **NOT** doing well? Where do they need help? Where are they having trouble? What are the problems?

This will take some time and some trust. It is challenging to develop a safe, non-threatening atmosphere for someone to share the difficulties of their ministry, but if you authentically care for these people, you will open the door to honest sharing. Let's face it—it's easy to spot a fake.

Don't fake it - Be real.

This is where mission work becomes effective.

Discover the "**Burden**" of a local church or ministry and assist in areas where they are not able to help themselves, while at the same time encouraging them to continue in carrying the "**Load**" where they are doing a good job. Once you discover where your help is needed, you can design a team to return and address those issues. You may discover that the local schoolteachers need training, or that there is NO ministry to men or the elderly, or that there are health issues requiring a medical team. Maybe they want to do a mime, skit or puppet show to attract kids to their summer program, but they never did a mime, skit or puppet show and have no idea where to start.

Once you discover what they need help with, you may have a reason to go back. Maybe you realize that the needs they have are not in your wheelhouse of possibilities. They may need a medical team, but you are just not equipped to help them in that area. **Great**! You have done your homework and you can now recommend this to a group that is qualified with medical teams.

☐ **Two - The Experiential Trip.**

You may have a group that has never had a cross-cultural experience. There is a great need within our churches for people to get out of their comfort zones and step out in faith. This is a true and viable need that translates well into a reason to take a trip. The concept is a good one; let us take a team to a foreign country to visit a missionary or indigenous ministry. We will see the work that they do, experience a different culture, and begin to understand some of the dynamics of foreign mission work. The team members will then be better equipped to pray for and financially support the work they see. If the missionary is someone your team knows well or was originally sent from your church, they may feel encouraged and valued because of your visit and fellowship.

However, there is great danger if the Experiential trip is incorrectly promoted as "Deep, serious, in the trenches, life changing mission work." Somewhere between the sight seeing and shopping the "In the trenches" part is just lost. The Experiential trip must be promoted and explained as just exactly what it is. It can be a very successful trip if the team learns to spread the vision, enlist prayer support, and generate giving.

Putting the experience in context by traveling to see some of the country, going to a local market, and eating at some local restaurants is important. But if they go home thinking they just changed the world and were involved in the nitty-gritty of mission work, the trip is a failure. The Experiential trip is very important and must happen before deeper ministry can take place, but it must be promoted and implemented as just that—an "Experiential Trip!"

☐ **Three - The Physical Trip.**

This trip is designed to meet some physical needs on the mission field. Typically this would be a builder's team or a sports outreach team. There are times when there are physical needs in the mission field that can only be met by sending in a team to do some work. Most of the time the local people in the area are better at building in their context than we will ever be. It is their community, their climate, their building materials, their tools, and their building techniques. In such cases we need to become the assistants and help the local worker to succeed with the project. Sometimes we are the experts. I have led teams with electricians because the goal was to properly wire a building for electrical service, and there were no local tradesmen capable of the task. So we took the lead, but we still worked alongside the local people shoulder to shoulder.

We have taken sports teams into Nicaragua to help a local church that wanted to reach out to its community with a sports program for the boys but they did not know how to organize or run it. We supplied the know-how, and made a lot of mistakes along the way. Then we adjusted our approach to match the context of the culture and community. With the help of the local churches we developed a successful ministry to boys. The greatest achievement was working with the young leaders of the church and equipping them to carry on the program without us.

☐ **Four - The Teaching and Training Trip**

If the main or core beliefs are solid, there may be a need to help develop "Depth" in the teaching, preaching and leadership of the local church or ministry. Do not go to the mission field just for the excitement of preaching your five favorite sermons to a new crowd who has never heard your jokes! Go with the purpose of helping them become better preachers and teachers. In some of these areas you will find that pastors are full of faith and commitment, but low on formal Biblical training. There is a need to help establish and strengthen the Biblical foundation of our churches everywhere, and that need is great in some areas of the world where mission work is being done.

As you may have noticed the types of trips we are talking about get deeper into ministry as we go on. The Survey trip accomplishes little or no ministry. The Experiential trip scratches the surface of ministry and gets the ball rolling. The Physical trip actually has "Hands On" ministry and the development of relationships. Then the Teaching and Training trip can take place after some trust has been developed. Being able to shape the minds and thought processes of leaders is a serious and powerful responsibility and privilege, so we must not take that lightly. We must earn the right to be heard and taken seriously. When we are given the platform to preach, teach, or share our testimony, we have been given the opportunity to speak truth with the authority of Scripture.

This is powerful and life-changing ministry; let us proceed with care and excitement.

☐ **Five - The Trip to the Trenches.**

This trip is hard to explain. Many years ago a good friend of mine married another good friend of mine. It was wonderful. It was a year later when the new bride became pregnant and there was great rejoicing. She carried the baby full term, but after some long hours of hard labor, the little baby was stillborn. He never took his first breath. He died sometime during the birth process. My friends requested that I do the funeral service. That was the most difficult funeral service I had ever done. I had extremely close ties to both families.

What an honor it was to be the conduit of comfort and assurance to a hurting family at a difficult time—to have the opportunity to turn the attention of those consumed with grief to the Lord—the giver of all comfort and peace. It was one of the most difficult things I was ever asked to do. However there was nothing I would rather have done.

Today there is great rejoicing in that family! There were five more pregnancies, and five awesome, healthy boys have been born into the family of my good friends, and these parents never take one moment with any of their children for granted.

The **Trip to the Trenches** is a little like that. This trip is truly in the trenches with the people you have come to serve. After you have spent years cultivating good, solid relationships, and you have proved your authentic concern, compassion and love for your partners in ministry, the trenches come alive!

There are times of great pain; when church discipline is needed, or a teenage girl you have worked with for years becomes pregnant out of wedlock and drops out of school – or worse – has an abortion, or a pastor you have been mentoring becomes unfaithful to his wife, or financial discrepancies are uncovered, and so on.

These are very hard things to deal with, but what would you rather do? Abandon your friends at the time of their greatest need? It is time to **Move the Stone** so there is nothing standing between Jesus and the people you have come to care about. You might be alone as a leader handling this deep ministry challenge, or you may need to assemble some faithful assistants to help and pray through to victory. You may be called on to lead the way to victory, but more probably you will need to assist the leaders within the biblical authority structure that is in place already. You made sure that authority structure was sound before you got involved years ago, so now it is time to stand on the security of Biblical principles to discipline and restore wayward sheep. That is the job of the local ministry or church you have been helping, but you **ARE** part of the fabric of their ministry because of the relationship you have developed with them, so be ready to be a participant in a painful but God honoring process.

And there is also great rejoicing! When the first female student from her small community to ever graduate from University walks across the stage to claim her diploma, because you prayed for her faithfully, supported her and wrote letters to encourage her, this is the time to rejoice. When the marriage of a church Elder is restored—against all odds, it is a time of rejoicing. How about when that girl who had entangled her life in all sorts of immorality and multiple abortions turns her life over to Jesus and marries a good man? She now has three kids of her own and is a testimony to the faithfulness and restoration power of Our Lord— rejoicing is sweet! What would you rather do? Go shopping?

Whatever the reason for your trip, **be clear about it**. Do not disguise a survey trip as a builder's trip, or a cross-cultural experiential trip as a teaching trip. This will frustrate those you intend to help, and set up unrealistic expectations for your team members. The **REASON** for the trip must be clear—at the very least to the LEADERS! On every trip with multiple team members there will be several things happening at the same time. **Don't miss this**. If there are 12 people on your builder's team, the main focus of the team is to help the local people accomplish a physical building task.

The team must remain focused on that task. However, you have asked another Pastor from your hometown to join you on this trip to check it out and see if he would like to partner his church with your church in future mission outreaches. For this Pastor the trip is more of a **Survey** trip—even though he will be helping with the building.

Then there are two team members who have never been out of the country before. Although they will be assisting with the building because they have some skills in that department—this is more of an **Experiential** for them.

The bulk of your team may be focused on the physical aspect of the trip, but you will be there on a Sunday and you have been asked to have someone preach at the local village church. Someone will have the deep honor of steering the congregation through the Scriptures on Sunday and that is no small thing. So **Teaching and Training** will be a part of your trip for at least one person.

And finally, while you are there a tragedy takes place in one of the local families you have known for years, and you are called on to minister at a level where only close friends and family are ever allowed. You enter the **Trenches** to bring comfort and order to a family in chaos, and the rest of your team stays back and prays. But this is a builder's trip! Without the core **REASON** to bring a team and faithfulness to that reason, these other aspects of the trip can never transpire.

Without a clear purpose to go, the trip has little chance for true success. If we understand the real needs of the mission field we are visiting, we can design an approach that will truly advance the cause of the Gospel, bless the local believers, and ensure a fulfilling trip for the team members now, and in the future.

Chapter Four
Come Back Soon

Non-Negotiable #2

I called a missionary friend of mine one day and when he answered the phone he sounded terrible. I asked him if he was sick and if everything was all right. He assured me he was fine—but exhausted. He said, "We just had a 20-person mission team here for two weeks. We just got rid of them yesterday and I hope I never see any of them again!"

I have also heard that same sentiment expressed in many different ways from missionaries and indigenous church leaders in other parts of the world. Based on these comments, and my own experience, I have come to believe that the following statement is true.

"God does not do short-term mission trips."

Yes, you read that right.

I firmly believe that God will have nothing to do with short-term mission trips. Instead, I am convinced that God is only interested long-term mission projects.

The only mission project that exists in the eyes of God is the long-term mission of reaching the lost with the Gospel of Jesus Christ.

We are commanded to *"Go... to all nations, baptize...teach"* Matthew 28:18. This is no short-term project. There are mission fields established all over the world with the goal of reaching the lost for Christ. The long-term mission plan impacts lives for eternity...

ETERNITY!

Now that's really long-term! God uses the short-term trips to SUPPORT the long-term goal of bringing salvation to Jerusalem, Judea, Samaria, and the uttermost parts of the world.

The so-called "short term" mission trip is not a mission trip at all if it does not fulfill the purpose of supporting the long-term mission of the great commission. Matthew 28:19 does not say "Go, shop, sightsee, have fun, get a tan, see the world, enjoy the adventure, and I will be with you through the end of the trip!"

Not at all. Jesus tells us,

"All authority in heaven and on earth has been given to me. Go therefore and make disciples of all nations, baptizing them in the name of the Father and the Son and the Holy Spirit, teaching them to observe all that I have commanded you. And behold, I am with you always, to the end of the age." (Matthew 28:19-20 ESV)

There are people who take that commission very seriously.

We call them missionaries, and national workers, church planters and ministry leaders.

That commission is a serious and difficult command. The ramifications of that command are plainly set forth in the Gospel of Mark where it says,

"Go into all the world and proclaim the Gospel to the whole creation. Whoever believes and is baptized will be saved, but whoever does not believe will be condemned."
(Mark 16:15-16 ESV)

Let there be no mistake, those who do not believe are already condemned by their sinful nature and they continue to be condemned when they do not believe.

The wonderful mission God has called us to is helping people escape the condemnation they deserve, and receive the salvation that is available to them "by grace... through faith" in Jesus Christ (Eph. 2:8).

If our short-term trip is focused on the command to reach the lost and support the work of those who are on the front lines of fulfilling that command, then our short-term trip is a vital part of the long-term mission of bringing salvation to the world. If our short-term trip is focused on the adventure of the team, the trip cannot be considered a mission trip. It is a vacation making believe it is a mission trip.

Non-negotiable #2:
Be a Blessing and not a Burden

The short-term team must be a blessing to and not an added burden on the missionaries and mission field they are visiting. One of the first overseas trips that I was a part of had people from several churches and was coordinated by a large mission board. One of the experienced leaders who had been involved with missions and leading trips for over 3 decades said this: "I have found that the best tour guides are the missionaries!"

For over 30 years this leader had been using missionaries as tour guides for his friends and groups traveling all over the world. Since this person was from the home office of the Mission Board—the missionaries always complied and made sure the team had a great trip.

No wonder I sensed a less than welcoming attitude from the missionaries when we arrived at their base of operations. But what had been accomplished for God on all of those short-term trips?

Very little I am afraid.

Short-term mission teams need to support the work of the missionaries in the field to further advance the work of the gospel. One of the ministry objectives of the team should be to encourage the missionaries who are far from home and often alone in a difficult work.

The support and encouragement from the short-term team should ultimately make the work of the field missionaries easier, not harder. The team needs to take care of their own housing, food, transportation, entertainment, counseling, and all other related costs.

The field missionaries will be happy to facilitate the team as they work together to build the kingdom of God. Obviously, the missionary or indigenous church leaders will need to help set up and make arrangements for housing, meals, and other plans for the team. They will be excited to do their part when they know the team is coming in to solve problems and give assistance where it is truly needed.

Early in my mission experience I traveled to Cuba for 10 days. I was with a small group that was led by a man and his wife from a large mission board. I noticed that our team always ate meals together, and our hosts would eat afterward. One evening I noticed that our host family did not eat anything after we finished. I spoke to one of the children to find out why, and found out that they did not eat because there was nothing left after our team had finished eating!

I spoke to our team leader about this situation and he remarked "We have given of our time and paid our way down here to minister to these people spiritually, the least they can do is feed and house us!"

I was horrified. He had made **NO** provisions for us to pay for the food and housing costs for our team while we were in Cuba. He just expected the local people to supply those needs. Unfortunately, these were very poor people, and food was scarce, so these loving people gave us what they had and went without eating themselves!

Once I realized what was happening, that our team was a major burden on this family, I prevailed over the team leader's objections and we all paid for our food and any expenses our team incurred. This included having the family eat WITH us for all of our meals. The team leader was not pleased, however our hosts were greatly relieved and they are still friends of mine to this day.

This may seem like an extreme case, but I assure you that it is not.

This happens all the time.

Some missionaries and indigenous churches refuse to have mission teams visit them because they cannot financially afford to have them there. It is expensive to supply transportation, housing, and the many other needs of a team.

Do not burden those you came to minister to.

Teams **MUST** pay their own way.

Having said that, I took a team of six men experienced in construction to Spain to work on a church building where they needed our expertise in certain areas in order to ready the building for the initial opening. The local church members (mostly women) decided that since they were not skilled in the areas that they needed us to work in, they would partner with us by supplying all of our meals for us! They wanted to be involved in the project but did not have the skills needed. We attempted to pay for the food supplies, but the church members would take nothing from us. They insisted on supplying our meals. Those were some of the very best meals I have ever eaten. And we were able to form a lasting partnership that still exists today.

I am sure you can see the difference in these two situations. Please be sensitive to the people you are ministering to.

In Cuba we would have been a tremendous burden to our host family if we had let them continue supplying our food.

In Spain, if we insisted on paying for our food we would have seriously offended the church members. They had sufficient finances and were trying their best to be part of their own church renovation project. WE were supplying some special skills that were needed, and THEY were supplying food that was needed.

We were in Estonia with a builder's team back in the early 1990s. Because of the local town ordinances, no work on the building was permitted on Saturdays and Sundays. So unexpectedly we found ourselves with a Saturday off. It was early July, and Saturday happened to be the 4th of July. We were invited to a local church member's house for a barbeque to celebrate our holiday, and spend time with them and their kids.

We noticed that this was that one special house in the neighborhood where all the kids gravitated. But the kids would hang out for a while and then run off to play somewhere else. The homeowner remarked that he had seen a picture of something called a "swing set" in a magazine and had always wanted to build one in his yard but had no idea where to begin or how to do it. He had never built anything before.

He and his wife wanted to attract the kids, give them something to do, and give him and his family an opportunity to minister to the kids and hopefully share the Gospel with the neighborhood families. That was all my team needed to hear. One team member sat with the homeowners and their kids and helped them come up with a design.

Another team member drove to the supply yard to price out materials. Within an hour we had a plan and a budget. The homeowner did not have enough money to pay for the project, and we had no time to develop a fund raising program for them to earn the money on their own, and my team only had that afternoon available to build it.

The team and the homeowners pooled their money together and purchased enough wood for the project. My team, the homeowner and his kids, along with some of the less shy neighborhood kids, spent the rest of the day working together—and laughing a lot!

By the end of the day there was a beautiful swing set, with a raised clubhouse and sandbox prominently situated in the back yard. The homeowners were close to tears, and their kids were exuberantly playing in the yard with scores of neighborhood kids. For years that swing set was the catalyst for much outreach work in that neighborhood, and many came to Christ because of that afternoon project.

A very important aspect of this project was what the kids were saying to their friends as they were invited over to play that evening; "Come over and play on the swing set that WE just built!" They did NOT say, "Look at the swing set that the Americans built for us!" After all, it was their idea, their design, they worked at it (and they had more than a few splinters and banged thumbs to prove it!), and they put their own money into it. They owned it—but we had the privilege of helping them accomplish something that they were not able to do themselves.

If this swing set adventure had been in a movie made in the United States, the story would have been quite different. After seeing scores of children in the neighborhood with no safe place to play, the team would have spent the day relaxing, and just watching and listening. Then, secretly, with great passion and self-sacrifice, they would have designed and built a fabulous swing set during their last days in the country at an undisclosed location. Late on the night before they were to fly out of town, they would have slipped into the homeowner's yard, installed the swing set without being detected, and been gone before the light of day. The homeowners would have awakened to the sound of joyous children playing on the incredible swing set now prominently on display in the yard, and the hero Americans would have been safe on the plane on the way home with no chance of being thanked for their incredible act of service!

This is not so different from the type of situation that Robert D. Lupton describes in his book "Toxic Charity" published by Harper One, where some well-meaning North Americans installed a much needed water well in a very poor village. It was great until the pump broke. No one fixed it. It was NOT the vision of the townspeople to have the well. They just went back to their old ways, walking miles to the river to bring less than clean water back to town.

Another poor village did develop a vision for a water well on their own. It was researched, funded and built with local vision and labor. Guidance and some financing was supplied by North Americans to get it started, but the entire project was a local effort that resulted in a community water utility company that was serviced and maintained and paid for by the local townspeople. What a great success!

Sometimes we try too hard to be heroes.

It is programed into us by our culture and worldview.

But there are better ways to be a blessing.

There are many trained missionaries and local ministry leaders that think of short-term teams in terms of "How much will we get from that team?" or "What will they give us next time?" or "When they come back I hope they bring more candy, or clothing, or gifts, or money," or whatever we have won them over with. There is an old saying that certainly has proven true over the years:

"Whatever you win them with, That is what you keep them with."

In other words, if a group has developed a relationship with a missionary or local ministry based on their ability to bring them gifts, they will need to keep bringing those gifts to maintain the relationship. Most likely they will damage or lose the relationship when they do not bring those gifts. The foundation of that relationship will crumble when the gifts, finances, work teams, or other "hero" activities slow down or stop. If the group has been giving these gifts in expectation that the missionaries and local ministries will show the group a good time, we have a **lose/lose** situation.

1) We teach indigenous ministries to be dependent on us, training them to look at North Americans with an attitude of "What can I get from them?"

LOSE

2) We train our teams to believe that real mission work is like a fun vacation: hard work is sometimes done, but the focus is on the "Enhanced Experience" of the team.

LOSE

This problem is compounded as we look to bigger projects.

I was working with a pastor in Africa who wanted to plant a church. He had a plan that he shared with me. He came to my office in New York and spread out blueprints for the church building he was planning to build. He was asking us to fund it. Well, the building he was planning to build had a sanctuary **LARGER** than the sanctuary in my church in New York, and I was serving in one of the bigger churches in the area!

He wanted to **start** his ministry with a building bigger than most pastors ever dream about having. **WHY**? He told me the reason. In his part of Africa many North American mission organizations were coming in to plant churches. The formula or pattern they used was this:

1) **Build** the biggest, most beautiful church building in the area.
2) **Purchase** a top-notch sound system, along with all types of high quality musical instruments.
3) **Hire** professional musicians and sound techs (their faith is unimportant).
4) **Open** the biggest, most beautiful church in the area with the best, loudest and most professional worship team available.
5) **Yell** a lot from the pulpit to get everyone excited.

Well, if the way a pastor chooses to win people is by having the biggest, fanciest, loudest, most professional, most exciting church in town, he will only be successful until another pastor or mission board comes into the area and builds a bigger, fancier, louder, more professional, and more exciting church! He will always need to be the biggest, fanciest and loudest in town if he wants to keep the people he won by being big, fancy and loud.

I advised this African pastor friend to try something radically different.

Win people with the Gospel of Jesus Christ!

Preach Jesus and develop authentic believers. Usher the life changing grace and mercy of the Lord into their lives. **Move the Stones** that are blocking the path to Jesus. Then what will he need to do to keep the people he has won by preaching the Gospel?

Keep preaching the Gospel!
Keep Moving Stones!
Keep proclaiming the truth!
Stay the course with faithfulness!

Give Jesus the glory, and the Lord will build the church.

It has been over ten years since that conversation with that African Pastor. It took ten years to retrain his worldview of church planting. He is now back in Africa planting healthy churches... not with beautiful buildings, not with sound systems, not with fancy singers but by winning the people with **THE GOSPEL**!

If you build your vision of missions on being the biggest, most beautiful team with the nicest gifts to give out, then you will only keep your relationships by always being the biggest, most beautiful team with the nicest gifts to give out.

So when we talk about being a blessing to the missionary and not an added burden, we must balance our activity so we do not fall into the ditch on either side of the road.

We can easily travel to the mission field with the best of intentions, but become a distraction and economic burden to the very people we are trying to help. We can spend our efforts in the mission field for two weeks, and when we leave—the work of the Lord has been hindered rather than helped. The local ministry leaders have been too overwhelmed to minister to their people because they were taking the team zip lining through the jungle, or shopping at the market, or counseling team members! (More about counseling team members later).

Or we can go to the mission field with the over enthusiastic purpose of blessing all those we come in contact with. In so doing, we bring the burden of our culture of western materialism as we push our benevolent gifts on those who would be better off without them. Or worse yet, sometimes our gifts take away their much-needed opportunity to work and feel the satisfaction of earning the money to supply their own needs.

This middle of the road is often hard to maintain. The wisest and most careful sometimes make mistakes and end up in a ditch on one side or the other regardless of how much experience they have and how much they understand and try to avoid problems. But if the group consciously tries to meet the real needs that form the reason for the trip, and do so with a servant's heart, great things happen in spite of the mistakes.

This becomes a **Win/Win** situation.

1) The missionaries and indigenous ministries get help where they really need it. The **REASON** for the trip is fulfilled.

WIN

2) The team gets a glimpse of what real mission work is, and a chance to develop a vision and authentic relationships with those in the field.

WIN

I have always wanted to be the team that people are sorry to see leave when the trip is over. I want the missionaries and local church people to think something like "Boy am I tired, but I feel great. We accomplished so much for the cause of the Gospel, and God was glorified while that team was here. We feel connected to others in the Body of Christ, and I think they really understand us and care for us. **I hope they come back soon.**"

Chapter Five
The Connection

Non-Negotiable #3

The three most common questions I receive from team members, their spouses and their parents as they sign up for a trip are:

1. Is there Internet?
2. Is there Wi-Fi?
3. Will my phone work?

I have developed a communication policy for all trips:

1) They can contact those at home when they get to their final destination to let their concerned loved ones know that they arrived safely.
2) They can contact their concerned loved ones at the halfway point of the trip to confirm that they are still OK.
3) They can contact their concerned loved ones the night before the team leaves the mission field for the trip home to remind those at home that they ARE coming home and DO NOT rent out their room!

I always make sure the family has the ability to contact the team leader in case there is an emergency at home and they need to get in touch with someone on the team, and we certainly do contact the people at home if someone on the team becomes sick, injured, or the situation requires it.

We are not unreasonable, but that is not good enough for some people. We live in a world today where instant availability is insisted on.

If a parent cannot reach their child on their cell phone immediately they panic and think the worse has happened.

People are accustomed to instant information, instant news as it happens, and instant relationships.

The "need to know" and the "need to stay connected" are consuming addictions that can stunt growth and development while isolating and distracting people from real connections with other people.

I have had team members constantly on the phone or text or skype or whatever at every possible moment when they get a signal or Wi-Fi connection. Usually that happens in the evenings, but sometimes it is a distraction **ALL DAY**!

What's the problem?

Aren't we supposed to stay connected to people back home so they can pray for us?

Well first let's look at a few practical problems. I have had team members call home and complain about being sick, while telling the team leader that they are fine. That just pits those at home against the leaders.

One hot summer day I had a member of a team become a little faint and nauseous out on the soccer field. This individual called home while sitting in the middle of the soccer field and was diagnosed with appendicitis over the phone by a family member! This all happened before the team leader was notified. The family member managed to call the local hospital in Central America from the US and talked to a doctor.

The "sick" team member spent 3 days and $2500 in the hospital because of what turned out to be a slight case of dehydration. All very avoidable!

First speak to the team leader, an assessment will be made, a doctor will be contacted if necessary, and family will be called if needed. We don't take chances with the health of our team members, but it is impossible for someone else to manage the health of a team member from 5000 miles away. Well, those things do happen but not frequently.

The bigger problem is less discernable.

Team members and people at home think it is awesome to get daily reports from the field and up to the minute news on ministry events. However, something less than healthy is going on. There is a problem with the team member who leaves home, travels to another part of the world but stays in constant contact daily with those at home.

What is the problem?

The problem is this: their body has gone on a mission trip but their brain remained back home!

Sound silly, well it happens! I have had people with me on two-week trips, who miss the entire trip because they were so concerned about the happenings back home that they were never able to enter into the trip.

I had one girl whose boyfriend decided to break up with her by text on the day we arrived in a foreign country. She spent the next two weeks consumed with trying to win him back or punish him for his deed and she missed the entire trip.

This is not just a younger generation problem. I have had adults spend hours on the phone or in contact with people at home every night. All day they take photos or videos to share each night. The entire trip for them revolves around the exciting report they send back home each evening.

There is great value in disconnecting from the normal routine of life and entering into another dimension of living in another context.

When we unplug from our electronic devices,
    from constant communication,
    from over stimulation,
    from information overload,
it is then – and **only then** that we can plug **into** God and what **He is doing in another culture or people group**.

When we **give our attention** to the job at hand—**a job that the Lord has called us to**—God expands our world and gives us new connections.

When we traveled to Cuba in 1997, there was no communication possible with home. We made arrangements with a woman in a town about 5 miles away. She had a phone, the only one in town. People would line up outside her home in hope of using her phone for a small fee. She was our emergency contact. If someone back at home in the US had an emergency and needed to contact a team member, they would notify someone on my home staff, they would call this woman in the little town in Cuba, she would run up the hill to the home of the local pastor, and he would send his son to get me 5 miles away. Well, that was great—and it worked surprisingly well! It forced the teams to disconnect from home, work, family, church, and everything else for two weeks. The entire team would enter into the culture, context, life style, and pace of life in Cuba, and live just as those we were there to partner with.

It was excellent!

On one trip we took a group of fourteen, which included 7 high school students, to Cuba for two weeks. The flight had a stopover in Miami for several hours, and for the entire duration of travel these high school students were glued to their phones. There was little or no interaction between team members, and no real unity. Once we landed in Cuba the cell phones were useless. Suddenly there was no place to hide. No distraction, no information, no news, no social media, no entertainment, and **no excuses**.

After a few days of grumpy withdrawal, every student entered into the trip with great energy. Suddenly they were interacting and talking with each other, and developing relationships with our Cuban partners. With no distractions to deter them, these members entered into the trip with a high degree of energy, and a major social transformation took place.

It resulted in a great trip. Sadly on the trip back home, as soon as we hit Miami the phones came out and the isolating distractions took over and we saw the new relationships that were formed on the trip among team members just fade away.

It is important to remove the distractions that stop or hinder our personal contact with others because the third non-negotiable in a short-term mission trip is:

Non-Negotiable #3:
There must be connection with local people

It is so easy for us to travel to the mission field as a team and never leave our little North American bubble. We stick together as a group, eat as a group, stay in hotels as a group, speak our language as a group, visit tourist restaurants, log onto Facebook, text and call home every day, and generally do our own thing while in the middle of a community that needs and wants a relationship with us.

The incredible Church of Jesus Christ is made up of many parts. The Apostle Paul explains this very well in 1 Corinthians 12.

Each part is unique and valuable to the rest of the body. It is a good thing when the hand has a close working relationship with both the foot and the eye.

The foot, hand and eye all need each other and help each other be better at their particular function. The foot runs better when the eye can see where it is going, the eye sees better when the hand wipes the sweat and dust away from the brow, and so on.

"You are the body of Christ"

Would we ever consider having one room where all the hands would gather, and another room where all the eyeballs would roll around, and another room where the feet would stomp together? That would be silly.

But we **WILL** keep in our North American bubble as much as we can, avoiding any real contact or meaningful interaction with the other parts of the Body of Christ.

I was on a trip to a very poor country with a team of teachers for two weeks, and another team from North America overlapped a few days with us. That team was scheduled to do some work projects. We had a two-day break before we continued with the next teaching seminar, so the director of the local ministry we were working with asked if we would assist the other team with their work project. I am always looking to make connections so we agreed. The project they had for those two days was to paint a large chain link fence belonging to a church in a very poor town. OK, no problem.

When we got to the jobsite we saw that the fence was totally overgrown with vines. The vines would need to be removed by hand before any painting could take place. This proved to be VERY labor intensive. The team worked hard for about an hour and made very little progress.

There was a group of 20 or so kids standing in the church yard just watching us. I first checked with the local pastor of the church to get permission, and then I asked the kids if they wanted to help us take the vines out of the fence so we could paint. They got excited and jumped at the opportunity to help.

I made teams of 3 or 4 mixing the kids with the adults and we all worked together. Some of the parents of the kids saw what was happening and came over to help. We had great fun, laughing and creating little contests to see who was fastest taking out the vines. Everything was well supervised and safe. The kids figured out a way to have one person on each side of the fence to work the same vine out and they were fast!

It took about four hours to clean all the vines out of the fence, but we could not have done it without the kids. Later that day we began to paint the fence, and the kids wanted to help again. It was a great time of working together and developing friendships.

I was looking forward to preaching at the church on Sunday and seeing the kids and parents again (Probably still with paint on their faces!) and building on the events of the day. It was a Home Run that was stretched out of a bunt single of painting a fence.

That evening when that large team gathered to have a team meeting, the team leaders addressed the group. They were not pleased with the events of the day. They had been with another part of their group at another location during the fence painting adventure. They heard all about the help the team received from the local kids and parents, and they told the group that interacting with the local people was strictly forbidden! They were there to get work done and **NOT** to work with the local people.

The group was told to stay by themselves and avoid contact with the "locals." The other part of the group that did some construction was **praised** because they did all the work by themselves and kept the "locals" away! What if one of those kids got hurt while pulling out vines? Our insurance won't cover that! What if they got paint on the only pair of pants they own?

I was shocked at what I heard.

Without contact with the local people, there is no mission trip. There is no purpose in going.

Just stay home.

Send $500 and hire a local to paint the fence.

At least some poor worker will earn some wages and the work will get done better and cheaper. Can you imagine Paul the Apostle having a "no contact with locals" policy on **his** mission trips?

We **MUST** develop friendships and relationships with others if we hope to be effective in the ministry God has called us to. God's most precious possession is His people. We know that because He died on the cross for His people. He has given us the opportunity to establish a bond with His most precious possessions in other parts of the world.

A good illustration of this comes from Nicaragua. I have been traveling there with groups for many years and have developed a good relationship with a small church out in the country. One Sunday evening I was visiting that church with my team and doing some teaching, and I was asked to stay after the service and sit in with the leadership for a meeting. The meeting was pleasant and functional as the leaders discussed church business issues. I felt privileged to be invited into the leadership circle and realized that I had somehow earned their trust.

The talk got around to repairing the roof. This church also had a school that consisted of two long buildings, one on each side of the church building, containing classrooms and offices. The school buildings desperately needed a new roof. The wood rafters were rotted and termite infested, and the corrugated steel had holes and gaps that let a tremendous amount of rain in to the classrooms. After discussing the problem for a little while they turned to me for advice.

I suddenly realized why they had asked me to their leadership meeting! They knew of my background in construction and they needed a new roof on their school and did not know where else to turn. I proceeded to ask a few questions and learned that they had been trying to raise money for the roof for several years. Each time they built up a sum of a few hundred dollars, something more urgent or more important came up and the money was used for that other purpose. This is an extremely poor area in Nicaragua, and I realized that they had been trying hard to solve their own problem. Now they were turning to me.

Only, I was not willing to take responsibility for their roof! The last thing I need is to design and build a new school roof in Nicaragua, and have them call me a few years later and say, "**YOUR** roof is leaking. Come back and fix **YOUR** roof!" And I told them so! I said, "I am not going to solve your roof problem. This is your roof. You need to solve this problem." I made it clear that this roof was their responsibility.

They were a little discouraged, but I continued. I laid out a plan for their roof that kept it **THEIR** responsibility. I laid out the following:
1) You get a local contractor to come in and design the needed roof.
2) He can be someone from the church, or from the community.
3) He must be able to design the new roof, and take responsibility for it and any problems that come up during the job, or after it is finished.

4) Get a full estimate for the materials and labor needed to complete this job.
5) Put a work team together of at least 12 men from your church and community to work on installing the new roof under the direction of the contractor.
6) If you do those 5 things, I will go back to my church and raise the money needed to cover the cost of the new roof.
7) I will come back with a team of 6-8 men to work **WITH** your men to install the new roof.
8) If I get here and you do not have 12 men to help, I will not give the money and I will not help. I will go home.

They began to get excited with the plan! By the end of the week I had in my hand a full estimate for the job, complete design sketches, and a commitment for 12 men to work on the roof. So I went home and raised the $8500 needed for the roof. I returned 6 months later with 8 men and $9000.

On the morning we gathered to start the job my team and I met the 12 men who were to help us, and the contractor. The contractor was a big man named Miguel, and he had his four workers with him. They were experienced welders, since the plan included all new steel rafters that needed to be welded in place. Miguel and his four workers all had a bit of an attitude when they met us. Miguel said to me "What do you want us to do?" And he just stood and waited. I replied, "You are in charge. You tell us what to do." He insisted that since I was paying them, I was in charge. I refused. This went on for a few minutes and became a stalemate.

I could not help but think that this contractor, Miguel, and his men must have worked with other North American teams who must have treated him and his workers poorly. I know they had their defenses up, expecting us to take charge. I finally turned to my team and the church workers and instructed them to sit down until the Miguel was willing to give us instructions. He was not ready for that. After a short conference with his four men he told me that the steel needed to be piled up in a certain area and primed.

I said, "Great, but first we pray". So I put one hand on Miguel's shoulder and prayed for protection for the contractors and all those working, and thanked Jesus for all His blessings. Miguel seemed a little surprised. I then put four men on that task and then said "Next?" He then told me that the old roof needed to be removed a certain way from one side, so I had six men help two of his men with the roof removal. And the rest of our men helped his other men remove the debris and cart it all out to a pile. Each of the men on my team and the men from the church followed the directions of Miguel and his men without comment. Miguel was obviously in charge of this job, and he was a very capable man.

The "attitude" we had seen earlier soon disappeared and we were all working hard, and sometimes laughing harder. That turned into a very good week. Miguel and his men were not Christians at all. During water breaks and lunch we began talking together and that first afternoon during our break I asked one of my men to give his testimony. He gave a 15-minute testimony, and then we all went back to work.

The next day, during our morning break, one of the Nicaraguan church men just started giving his testimony. At lunch the non-Christian contractors asked us to continue with the stories about our lives! So we continued all week, and those hardened contractors shared some details about their lives.

Every morning those contractors would wait until we prayed together before work started. We finished that roof in six days. When it was done the Pastor of the church and his congregation looked at the job and said, "Look at the new roof **WE** put on our school, with the help of Pastor Paul and his team." They did **NOT** say, "Look at the roof Pastor Paul and the North Americans gave us." They owned their own roof! We all became friends during that week. I got the opportunity to share the Gospel plainly with Miguel and his men. I do not know if they came to faith in Jesus since that time. They did not respond in an outward way, but they did say this to me; "If you ever need another contractor in Nicaragua, please call us! We like working with you. You people are.... different."

I like to think that the difference they saw in my team and the church workers was Jesus within us. I can only pray that the seeds that were planted will be watered by others and harvested by still others.

****

The culture in North America has changed drastically in the last few decades. The generation that fought in WWII was a generation that was "outward focused". They sacrificed a lot, and some sacrificed everything for their country, their family, their faith, and for others. That generation was looking outside of themselves to the good and betterment of others. Isn't that what Christ calls us to as we again look at the great commission;

Jesus came and said to them, "All authority in Heaven and on Earth has been given to me. Go therefore and make disciples of all nations, baptizing them in the name of the Father and of the Son and of the Holy Spirit, teaching them to observe all that I have commanded you. And behold, I am with you always, to the end of the age."
Matthew 28:18-20 ESV

We are told to **GO**!

Be outward focused.

Value others more than yourself.

That is what mission work has been for 2000 years, But after WWII the culture in North America began to change. It has made a complete 180 degree turn, and now North American culture is inward focused.

"What is best for me?"

We see that culture invading our churches and mission organizations. Mission trips are planned for the benefit and enjoyment of the team, not the lost souls.

Mission organizations advertise trips that promise teams a life changing experience and an adventure with a purpose, along with shopping and sightseeing in the most exotic lands.

In some circles of Christian missions the focus of mission work is **completely** focused on the team going on the trip, **not at all on the lost souls going to Hell**.

What Happened?

No interaction with local people! That's what happened!

- Too many cell phones
- too many phone calls home
- too much social media
- too many distractions
- too much sight seeing
- too much shopping
- too much focus inward

Soon the lost soul has no face.

They are right next to you painting a fence, but there is no interaction, no connection. What does that lost child look like? Facelessness is easy to ignore. Stay safe! Stay Isolated! Stay unconnected!

Sounds like a plan from the pit of Hell.

It is not the work we do in the mission field that makes the difference. It is the connections we make that Move the Stones and put people face to face with Jesus that makes the difference.

I know some of the real needs that short-term teams work through are very physical in nature, but that only paves the way for connections of the heart to take place at some level deeper than cement and brick.

Every soul has a face, every face has a person, and when that person comes face to face with Jesus, it's because someone took the time to **CONNECT!**

Chapter Six
"Day 10"

Non-Negotiable #4

Someone on the team is having a bad day! There is a painful trial they are going through, homesick, just plain sick, or people are getting on their nerves. They just want to hide – but can't!

Day 10 is the day someone runs out of deodorant, someone else runs out of clean clothes, another runs out of makeup, everyone is tired of rice and beans, and someone else runs out of patience. Someone breaks down, tempers flare, friendships are challenged, voices are raised, and we say,

"What is happening?"

All of the defense mechanisms are failing.

There is no car to jump in, no windows to roll up, no air conditioning to turn on—and no driving away. There is no private bedroom run to and no door to lock. No TV or loud music to get lost in, no gym to work out in, no job to get buried in.

There is no insulation of a busy schedule to keep the separation from God intact.

There is no place to hide!

They are stuck on this trip with God, and the team leader.

Excellent!

God has been waiting 10 days for this day to get here.

Non-Negotiable #4:
The Team Must Minister to Itself

It is possible that this is the first time God has ever had direct access to this individual's life without all of the distractions, defense mechanisms, escape plans, and the insulation of a busy schedule getting in the way. If someone is having a tough time on Day 10 it is possible that God has finally gotten their attention through this painful trial.

Now He wants to speak with them!

He wants to speak truth into their heart. He wants to enlighten their mind, build their character, administer correction, give instruction, supply training, and reveal Himself to them in a new and wonderful way. But He cannot do any of that until He moves them out of their comfort zone. Now that they are uncomfortable they are ready to hear what He has been trying to say to them, maybe for years! And, maybe that someone having a bad day and needing to listen to what God is saying—is YOU! So be ready to listen to Him! He is revealing Himself. He may be speaking through other people, or a situation, Scripture, or in other ways.

Pay attention today and expect God to show up. Don't miss it!

I tell all of my team members about Day 10. I tell them to expect a bad day when they come to the end of their strength. Sometimes that happens on Day 10 itself, sometimes a few days earlier or later. On longer trips it happens later, for instance, on a 3 week trip Day 10 happens on day 15 or so. On shorter trips I have been known to confiscate soap and deodorant in order to create a Day 10 earlier in the trip! (Only kidding!).

The concept of Day 10 is real and important regardless of what day the crisis manifests itself. So I tell my team members "When you come to me on Day 10 crying and upset, having a really bad day, complaining and discouraged, I will say, EXCELLENT!" I will ask them what God is trying to teach them. I will tell them to learn it now so they don't need to learn this lesson all over again. And then I work through the problem with the individual. I told them that Day 10 would come, so let's deal with it. God accomplishes His most powerful work in us when we are uncomfortable and suffering.

"Beloved, do not be surprised at the fiery trial when it comes upon you to test you, as though something strange were happening to you. But rejoice insofar as you share Christ's sufferings, that you may also rejoice and be glad when his glory is revealed." (1 Peter 4:12-13 ESV)

The team must be ready to minister to itself.

It is not the job of the missionary or local ministry leaders to handle the problems and issues developing on your team. Of course if someone gets hurt or sick, or an emergency situation occurs the missionary and local leaders will be more than ready to assist as needed. However, the team conflicts, interpersonal friction, individual breakdowns, personal crisis events, all should be handled within the team. That is why there always must be a "pastor" on the team. This is not always (and perhaps rarely) an official, ordained pastor, but there must be someone on the team who fills the role of pastor. This person must have the ability and motivation to shepherd the team in time of crisis, and minister to individuals in their time of need.

This team is an extension of the church, and ministry to the flock must continue, especially as these sheep are being led out of there secure surroundings and into new and strange territory. The role of pastor on the team is covered more fully in the next chapter, but it is important to know here that the dynamic of Day 10 is real and must be prepared for. The missionary and local leaders are not prepared or equipped to handle the problems on your team. That responsibility falls on the team leaders. Bear in mind, everyone is not expected to deal with everyone else's problems. "Group therapy" is rarely helpful and often destructive in these situations. The leader who is filling the role of pastor will need to deal with issues Biblically, appropriately, and often confidentially.

I have never had to send a team member home for behavioral problems, although I did come close once or twice. Sometimes an individual seems to set his or her sights on conflict and disruptive behavior. I have always been *willing* to remove the offending team member and send them home alone so as not to damage the rest of the team. That is not always an option depending on the trip location, length of trip, and so on, however it IS an option to be considered for the health and safety of the team. Having said that, the situation must be serious and actually warrant such action. Knowing that option exists is usually enough to keep any deliberate sabotage under control.

Knowing that there is likely to be a Day10 with regard to problems and considered "normal" is usually enough to help most team members deal with the issues that come up during an extended trip. But without someone in the pastor role ready to deal with problems, a small and insignificant situation can explode and threaten the success of the trip for one or all of the team members. Therefore, it is important that this person be prepared to shepherd the flock and take responsibility for the individuals on the team without putting an added burden on the missionaries or local leaders. We will never have a perfect team of problem free people. But we can have a perfect team of people who deal with their problems in a Biblical way and learn, grow and mature through the process. That does not happen by accident. Plan for it.

Most often the person or persons going through the Day 10 problem period need a safe place to work through the problem. They need someone to think clearly with them and steer them into the right thought process and plan of action. On one occasion, two of my good friends just exploded at each other. I decided the best course was to sit with each of them separately—and then bring them together. There needed to be a safe environment established for them to express feelings and frustrations. After dealing with the situation in a safe and open manner the solution became evident. With the guidance of Scripture they moved back to a solid relationship that included forgiveness and acceptance. Keeping them focused on Jesus was the key, and the time together ended with tears and a restored friendship.

Let us look at the error of taking something to the extreme. I know of mission teams being sent out that purposely include people with little or no faith in Jesus, have overwhelming life problems, and are extremely "high maintenance." They are sent on a trip to a foreign land in the hopes that the experience of the trip itself or the missionary they are visiting will straighten them out!

I have found in most of these cases there is no person filling the pastor role and no one is prepared to deal with the problems of these individuals. The missionary or local ministry leaders being visited must then spend a great amount of time and energy "putting out fires" for these people. The result of such a trip is most often a disaster. Missionaries and local leaders become overburdened and want nothing to do with future teams, and the team itself will often return home with no desire to embark on another mission trip ever again.

I deal with senior pastors who refuse to promote mission trips in their churches because of a terrible experience they or their church has had. I have also been on the receiving end of such teams. One team of 25 was sent to us for four days to perform drama and skits. None of the team members were believers in Christ! The organizers of the trip purposely assembled non-Christians and sent them on "tour" for a month, staying in the homes of church families. The hope was that these individuals would find faith in Jesus on the trip by being witnessed to by the families they were staying with.

However, the organizers never told us the plan!

We all thought these were Christians on a mission trip, looking to share the Gospel. NO WAY! This group was on a 30-day party trip. Families spent most of the 4 days policing the behavior of the team, which included sneaking out, drinking, drugs, and other immoral behavior. Unfortunately, this type of team is all too common on the mission field, and the team leaders never seem to be prepared to deal with the problems on their own team.

These types of teams are NOT mission teams!

This COULD be a tool to evangelize people through the dynamic of being on a trip. If that is something that is being attempted, then it should not be called a mission trip. These people are not missionaries spreading the Gospel or helping others to reach the lost. They ARE the lost!

If such a trip takes place, there MUST be leaders on the team to handle every aspect of oversight and outreach to these individuals. It can be very effective to take non-Christians on a trip outside their comfort zone to experience another culture, remove the distractions that insulate them from God, and guide their experience to a saving knowledge of Jesus. That would be more like an "Experiential trip" as described in chapter Three.

However, do not create a FAKE mission trip to do that. Do it openly, let those you visit know what is planned, and prepare the leadership team to handle ALL the dynamics such a trip will develop.

Once again, non-negotiable rule #4 must be adhered to; "The Team Must Minister to Itself"

Stand Firm

So how do we encourage our team at a time of crisis? How do we refocus the energy and commitment of the individuals we are working with?

Even the most seasoned travelers will fall into the pit of Day10 discouragement once in a while. How do we remove a problem from the focus point of an individual or group, and establish Christ clearly as the center of attention?

Let us explore one root of discouragement.

There is sometimes a question that creeps into our minds that can be the source of great distress. I do not know where this question originates. Is it a fiery dart from Satan used to discourage us? Is it a soul searching question from God used to search our motives and adjust our future efforts? We seldom ask this question when things are going well and we are encouraged. But when the going is tough, and we see little or no progress, when Day 10 hits, the question is all around us.

The Question: **"Am I making any difference at all?"**

Is our team making a difference with the mission we are on?

Are we making a difference in the lives we have connected with?

Will anything be different for the people we have interacted with because of the time we spent with them?

Was the cost for this trip with regard to money and time worth the result?

The question expands as we think—are we making a difference back at home? In my family? At work?

Am I making a difference **ANYWHERE**?

This is a haunting question that attacks us at our lowest points. We may never get the answer to this question while we are here on Earth. Why no answer? I have come to a realization that is simple yet profound. It helps me deal with this haunting question. The realization:

The fruit of my labor does not belong to me.
The fruit of my labor belongs to the Lord.

In the Gospel of John Jesus tells us,

"I am the vine; you are the branches. If a man remains in me and I in him, he will bear much fruit; apart from me you can do nothing." "You did not choose me, but I chose you and appointed you to go and bear fruit—fruit that will last." (John 15:5&16 NIV)

Without the Lord Jesus we can bear no fruit. It is only in Christ that we bear any fruit at all. And the fruit is all His! He chose us, He sent us, He bears fruit through us, and He receives the glory. This is eternal fruit "that will last". The fruit we bear for Christ will live in eternal glory with Him. He purchased the fruit with His blood on the cross at Calvary.

We are privileged to be workers of the harvest bearing that fruit into the kingdom. However, we may never see the fruit of our labor with our own physical eyes. Since the fruit belongs to the Lord and not to us, and since it is spiritual fruit, we may never see it here on this earth.

This can be discouraging to us. As humans we are accustomed to seeing and enjoying the fruit of our labors. We work hard and expect to earn wages, or we work to accomplish a task that we can step back and admire. We find it hard to continue working when we see little or no fruit. We like the feedback we get from successes and we want to know we are on the right track. God knows this. Sometimes the Lord gives us just enough insight into the fruit we are bearing to encourage us and keep us focused.

Sometimes we see NO fruit at all, and we must proceed on faith alone. We know that in the book of Hebrews it tells us:

"And without faith it is impossible to please him, for whoever would draw near to God must believe that he exists and that he rewards those who seek him".
(Hebrews 11:6 ESV)

I was once asked to join a meeting with a group of pastors in Central America where we have been working with local ministries for quite a few years. I was given a few days notice and was told the pastors in the local church association wanted to discuss the possibility of a future training session for pastors. I attended the meeting with the expectation of discussing future ministry plans.

After a few polite formalities, the leader of the group introduced me as the speaker of the pastor training session taking place NOW!

I was given 3 hours to speak truth into the lives of these 25 pastors RIGHT NOW! My translator looked at me in a panic, but we trusted God and stepped out in faith. I shared with them the concept of "The Load and the Burden" as contained in chapter Two. This is a cornerstone concept of our ministry and it applies to many aspects of the Christian life.

I finished the day with a question and answer time with the pastors. I went back to the house I was staying in and felt drained. I had received little feedback from the pastors, and I felt like a failure. I had gone to this meeting unprepared, no notes, and no plan of action. I had somehow misunderstood what they were looking for that day, and I was just shooting from the hip. I was discouraged with myself and just wanted to go home.

It was a major Day 10 experience for me.

We finished that trip well and many other things were accomplished, but that pastor training experience haunted me. I had been given an opportunity to pour into the lives of 25 eager pastors and I felt I had not made any difference at all.

Well, I travel to this area a few times a year, and about two years later after speaking at a church service, I was visiting with a few of the same pastors who had been at that training session. The leader of the Association of Pastors was there and suddenly began to tell me how the training I had given two years earlier had changed the way he was helping people in the community. Actually, it had changed his whole approach to ministry! Several other pastors chimed in and rattled off the main points of the message, and they spent about 30 minutes sharing successes on how the "Load and the

Burden" had helped them personally, in their ministry and their churches.

That pastor training session had been a great success! I was just unable to see any fruit at the time.

Two years after the training session the Lord showed me a little of His fruit that was brought into the warehouse on my watch. It was very encouraging and humbling. These pastors wanted more teaching to help them. This has led us to begin a pastor-training module where we bring in high level, trained teachers to pour into the lives of these precious local pastors who have very little formal training.

So how do we encourage our team when Day 10 is bringing them down? Scripture gives us some good instruction on this.

> *Therefore, my dear brothers, **stand firm**. Let nothing move you. Always give yourself fully to the work of the Lord, because you know that your labor in the Lord is not in vain."*
> *(1Corinthians15:58 NIV)*

Stand firm! Let nothing move us from the victory we have through our Lord, Jesus Christ. Our attitude must be one of standing in Christ, not our own feelings or desires. Our humanity wants to see the results of our efforts so we can feel good about ourselves. Instead we must receive our self worth from the fact that we have been saved by the blood of Jesus Christ. Stand firm in that.

When we stand firm in Christ Jesus with our attitude, words and deeds, and we give ourselves fully to the work of the Lord, we will then KNOW that our labor in the Lord is not in Vain.

We will not need to rely on our emotions to make us feel good, or seeing the results we desire to glory in. We can put our head on the pillow at night knowing that we have been obedient to the task given us, and that God has been glorified, and He gets all the credit. There is no limit to the things we can accomplish for the glory of God if we do not insist on getting the credit for ourselves.

With this concept of "STANDING FIRM" in the hearts of our team members, Day 10 problems just pass by and fade away.

We must Stand Firm on purpose!!

It does not happen by accident!

Let us prepare to turn Day 10 problems into eternal victories for the glory of our Lord, Jesus Christ.

Chapter Seven
The Disciples

Every team must have ten Disciples on it. There may be more or less persons on the team, and some may be duplicates. There must be a total of ten people. Even if there are five persons, ten disciples are needed.

This may sound a little odd, but it will make sense as I explain. There are ten different and distinct roles that need to be filled on any given team. Some of these roles are more evident than others, but they are all needed to have a successful mission trip. In this chapter each of the ten roles have been given a Biblical person to illustrate the characteristics of the necessary role. There is usually a need for someone on the team to assume multiple roles for the trip, just as in a family the father can be the father of the children, husband of the wife, repairman of the roof, and the cutter of the grass.

It is important to know the ten different people needed on the trip so that vacancies can be filled with purpose instead of by chance. The leader is most often the individual that must fill multiple roles as needed, but that can vary depending on the makeup of skills, talents and personalities on your team. The leader will need to delegate these responsibilities if they do not come about naturally.

Lets enjoy this adventure analyzing these ten disciples and their assorted personalities and duties.

1. Moses the Leader.

Every team needs a leader. This Moses must understand the need for this trip and push for it to happen. Moses told Pharaoh,

"Let my people go, that they may worship me."
(Exodus 8:1 ESV)

The leader is keenly aware of the "reason" for the trip (as we explored in chapter three) and is able to explain this reason to others. The leader of a mission trip knows there are many decisions he must make before any trip can be started:

A. WHY go on a trip?

At some point, like Moses, the leader must come to the realization that a trip is needed. It will be one of the five types of trips detailed in chapter One. This does not happen by itself. Without a Moses, the people are stuck in Egypt.

B. WHAT is to be accomplished?

In chapter 3 we discussed the reason for the trip. To the leader this reason must be crystal clear. Which of the five types of trips is it? A builder's team? A medical outreach? Survey? A combination? It is the leader who sets the objectives and expectations of the team in a realistic and Christ centered manner

C. WHO is the missionary you will visit?

Possibly there is a missionary that your church has been supporting for years and the time is right to go and help them in the field. Or maybe a mission agency has a need to assist one of the missionaries on their staff. There are a variety of other connections that might lead you to consider visiting a particular missionary.

Who is this missionary? What is their purpose for being on the mission field? Are they church planters? Evangelists? Medical missionaries? Are they training pastors? Are they married? Children? Denomination? Prayerfully deciding whom the missionary is that you are traveling to see is critical. Talk, research, ask questions, investigate, and get recommendations. Moses then makes a decision (usually with input from others).

D. WHERE to go in the world?

This will usually be decided when the missionary is chosen. However that is not always the case. I work with many churches and sometimes I am asked, "Where in the world do you need help?" Sometimes a church has an interest in a particular area of the world, and sometimes they have a ministry skill and are willing to use it anywhere in the world. God led Moses to the Promised Land and he will show the leader of the team where to go.

E. WHEN to schedule the trip and how long?

Don't go to Ghana, Africa in the rainy season to help build a building! The rain will wash away all of the cement you pour. Don't go to Nicaragua in June and expect to spend 2 weeks with kids at a summer camp. The kids are in school! Their summer vacation is December and January. The leader will consider the school, church and local community schedules and weather conditions on the mission field when setting up the dates for the trip, as well as scheduling a time when team members can participate.

F. HOW will funds be raised?

This is covered more fully in chapter eight. The leader works with the team, church leadership, the missionary, and others to determine the budget for the trip and how to raise funds. There are two aspects of this:

1. Expenses for individual team members.
2. Cost of the project or ministry being planned.

G. WHICH applicants will be chosen?

The leader must determine what characteristics and skill sets are needed in the individuals on the team. The Builders team will be a different group from the Medical team, and the pastor training team will be different again. What spiritual maturity level is required? What are the minimum and maximum ages? The leader is the one who oversees the processing of the applications.

"Obey your leaders and submit to them, for they are keeping watch over your souls, as those who will have to give an account. Let them do this with joy and not with groaning, for that would be of no advantage to you."
(Hebrews 13:17 ESV)

2) David the Shepherd.

King David was not always a King. He was first a shepherd. He was an excellent shepherd. The attitude, skills, temperament, and character that being a shepherd developed in David is most likely what prepared him to be King. We know he cared for his sheep in a protective way and he put himself in harms way several times to ward off danger and keep his sheep safe. He killed a lion and a bear to protect them, and I am sure he did many more brave deeds in the years he was a shepherd that were not recorded. (1 Samuel 17:34-36)

Every short-term mission team needs a David.

When "Day 10" hits, it is David that tends to the flock so that Satan does not get a foothold. It is David that helps the individuals on the team to deal with issues that God is addressing in their lives. It is David that looks after the spiritual wellbeing of each team member and is ready to protect him or her as they walk in unfamiliar territory. It is David that has his "spiritual radar" up and tuned in to danger, watching over even the most seasoned team members.

David is the shepherd of the team. He is the acting pastor. Not necessarily an official pastor, but filling that role for the team during the trip. His protective "pastor's eye" is always watching, and his ear is always listening for signs of turmoil. And when one of the sheep on the team needs to be disciplined, learn a difficult lesson, adjust their attitude, and respond to God, it is the Shepherd David that combines truth with love and cares for the individuals in need.

David does NOT turn his problem over to the missionary being visited in hope that the issue can be solved without him. David takes seriously the responsibility for shepherding the flock he has been given, and embraces the opportunity to help the sheep grow in faith and maturity. David creates a safe place for the team to learn, grow spiritually, and mature in the Lord.

I was leading a team in Central America with 16 people. On the team were 4 girls between 17-19 years old. On Day 10 there arose a problem between two girls. They had been good friends, but the pressure of the trip and the close contact for ten days was wearing on their friendship, and things began to fall apart. One of the girls began talking badly behind the back of the other. I called on both of them to work things out between them. Nothing worked.

The problem seemed to be centered on one girl who became vindictive when she could not control the other girls. That was something I would not stand for. I forced the issue, enacted discipline, and I informed her that she had one hour to do the right and Godly thing. She must make things right, apologize, forgive, and restore the relationship or I was going to put her on a plane back home that night.

That would have marked a great failure in her life. One hour later she came to me with the other girl and confirmed that she had done the right and Godly thing as I had instructed. There were no further problems with her for the rest of the trip. She was not very pleased with the pain and discipline I had put her through, but I was satisfied with the result. I figured that after the trip she would most likely avoid me and I would probably not see her again.

Two years later there was a knock on my office door and this girl came in. She had a problem and did not know what to do about it. A friend of the family had molested her and she did not know where to turn. She told me that she "knew I would do the right thing" so she came to me for help.

We confronted the offender in a Biblical way and the girl, her family and the church felt secure and protected. (And by the way, the individual received the help he needed). This girl and I have been good friends ever since and she comes to see me whenever she is in town. David is not afraid to shepherd his flock and push them to maturity.

"For everyone who lives on milk is unskilled in the word of righteousness, since he is a child. But solid food is for the mature, for those who have their powers of discernment trained by constant practice to distinguish good from evil." Hebrews 5:13-14 ESV

3) Paul the Preacher.

Paul the Apostle had the ability to preach a message anywhere, anytime, in any culture, under any circumstance, and glorify the name of our Lord Jesus.

There must be a "Paul" on the team, always ready to glorify the name of Jesus, whether given plenty of notice or called on at the last minute. This person does not need to be a professional preacher. It must be someone who is willing and able to share the Gospel and deliver a message as needed. It is best for the Paul on the team to have a few teachings with him on the trip knowing that there may be an opportunity to speak.

Simple, basic teachings that are easily translated are best. The simplest messages are the most powerful and will reinforce what they have already heard from their

110

own pastor. There is great value in hearing the same truth shared from different sources. Sometimes the message can be in the form of a personal testimony that gives glory to the Lord, and is culturally appropriate for the context of the trip. The personal testimony should have three elements:

1. The person's life before they were Christian. (Caution must be taken to NOT make the "Before I was a Christian" portion sound like a good time party and a great, sinful adventure. Tell the truth, but be sensitive. If those times included sinful addictions, the testimony should realistically portray that they were lonely, sick and terrible times. Details are not needed.)

2. How they met Christ and received their faith.

3. Their life since becoming a Christian.

This life testimony should be simple, yet contain stories of life events. This can easily take 20–30 minutes or more. With a translator—a little longer. This can be a great message for a Sunday morning, informal church gathering, or an impromptu opportunity to share on a jobsite or with a medical outreach patient. Actually, ALL team members should have their testimony ready to share on a one to one basis as opportunity arises.

"But in your hearts honor Christ the Lord as holy, always being prepared to make a defense to anyone who asks you for a reason for the hope that is in you. Yet do it with gentleness and respect." (1 Peter 3:15 ESV)

4) Joshua the Strategist.

Joshua was the military strategist. He organized the troops, prepared the people for battle, kept the objective in mind, and set his mind on accomplishing the task. Moses is the team leader and has set up the plan for the things to be accomplished. It is now up to Joshua to execute the plan that has prayerfully been decided upon.

The five types of trips discussed in chapter three each have different objectives and plans. And each of the five has variations in their objectives. Joshua is aware of all of this and is prepared to keep the team focused and on track. Distractions can derail a trip and destroy the objective. The job of Joshua in Scripture was to get rid of the Canaanites that were attempting to derail the plan of God. The overall objective of the Joshua on the team is always to glorify Jesus and testify of His Gospel. That is accomplished when the task at hand is completed with a Christ like attitude. Healthy relationships are then built or reinforced, and the testimony of Jesus is established.

A member of a builder team working in a small mountain village suggested they change their plans, cut short their involvement in the building project by a few days and let the local people finish the job by themselves. He wanted the team to have a 2-3 day adventure and hike up the mountain to a picturesque little village he heard about just on the other side of the mountain. This member distracted others on the team away from the task God had called them to. He distracted them with the lure of adventure! It was Joshua who kept the team focused on the task at hand. He called the team back to the original objective. The team joyfully stayed and finished the building project with the local people. As a result the project was finished, souls were touched, and a Bible believing church was established for the first time in that town. A Canaanite invasion was defeated!

In Central America during an exceptionally hot two-week trip, a team helping with ministry to children in a remote village was tired, uncomfortable, and ready to go home. The children from the community had been having fun every day with the team members and local church leaders, and that morning was no exception. The children were waiting expectantly in the field for activities to resume after lunch. But the team was in no mood to continue. The extreme heat had sucked away their energy, and flies had descended upon their lunch meal in a reenactment of the fourth plague in Egypt! The pungent smell from the city garbage dump situated right next to the school was carried in on every little breeze. The team was DONE! It was Joshua who took the time to re-focus the attention of the team away from themselves and back on the objective—glorifying Jesus—and set the attitude of each team member back on track. I don't remember what words Joshua said that day, but the team received a fresh perspective and a renewed vision! They finished the day, and the rest of the week with joy and purpose. As a result, many of those children entered a Christ centered scholarship program and their lives have been radically changed! Another Canaanite distraction defeated! Joshua knows he is at war, and he takes his command seriously.

> *"Only be strong and very courageous, being careful to do according to all the law that Moses my servant commanded you; Do not turn from it to the right hand or to the left, that you may have good success wherever you go." (Joshua 1:7 ESV)*

5) Jethro the Observer.

The father-in-law of Moses was a wise and observant man. Jethro watched Moses as he judged over the Hebrew people and he made suggestions that were very important and valuable. The delegation of authority used in our societies today is commonly called the "Jethro Principle". (Exodus 18:14)

This same kind of observation is needed on each mission trip. This is different from the observation that David the shepherd has as he watches over the flock of team members as discussed earlier. The observation of Jethro is over everything in a general sense. Jethro watches for the interaction between team members, as well as the interactions of the team members with the local believers and the indigenous people. Jethro watches the leaders of the local church and the missionaries to make sure they are satisfied with the ministry taking place with the team.

Jethro has a prayer he prays each day that goes something like this; "Lord, I know I can't watch everything that is going on, but will you please allow me to see the things I need to see. Show me good things that happen so I can encourage those who are involved. Show me the problems and potential pitfalls so we can avoid the pain of conflict and move the ministry to the next level of bringing honor to your name."

Jethro never talks behind the backs of people, whether team members, missionaries, leaders, or others. He brings his observations straight to Moses, the Leader, and a proper, biblical approach is taken to address any issues. Sometimes Jethro and Moses are the same person on a team. In that case, extra wisdom and caution are needed before major decisions are made.

Without Jethro on the team, Satan sneaks in where no one is watching and establishes a foothold.

"Oil and perfume make the heart glad, and the sweetness of a friend comes from his earnest counsel."
(Proverbs 27:9 ESV)
"Without counsel plans fail, but with many advisers they succeed." (Proverbs 15:22 ESV)

6) Martha the Worker.

Martha is often given a bad rap. In the story about Martha and Mary with Jesus, Mary is sitting at the feet of Jesus and Martha is working by herself to make all the preparations. She is undoubtedly cooking, cleaning, and setting up for the guests. She wants Mary to help her but Jesus tells Martha that Mary has chosen what is better. (Luke 10:38-42)

Well, does that mean that what Martha is doing is not important? Should she stop her chores and sit with Mary? Is Jesus suggesting that no preparations are needed? Well, someone needs to cook the meal, or they will all be hungry. Someone needs to clean the house, or everything will be dirty.

Without a Martha nothing gets done. Crops aren't planted, there is no harvest, no food, and society crumbles. Is Jesus saying it is better for us all to give up working and just sit at His feet? I don't think so. Scripture tells us,

"If anyone is not willing to work, let him not eat."
(2 Thess. 3:10 ESV)

Jesus simply says that Mary has chosen the better. Mary is consumed with Jesus while Martha is consumed with chores.

This leads us to a challenge. We are called to be part of a mission trip. The very nature of a trip requires that we accomplish something. There are chores to be attended to. We need Martha on this trip. Actually, we need several Marthas on this trip. There is a focus and objective that needs to be accomplished, and Joshua the Strategist must keep the team task oriented.

The members must be chosen for the team with the expectation that they can help fulfill the reason for the trip. The objective must be achievable with the skill set assembled within the team.

A builder's team should have Marthas on the team that have building skills.

A teacher training team should have Marthas on the team that have the skills to train other teachers.

A medical team must have trained Marthas that can perform the medical tasks required.

The team needs "Martha Workers," ready and able to successfully accomplish the task at hand.

However, if these Marthas are consumed by the task, they will miss the better part—Jesus! Martha must learn to accomplish the task or chore with the attitude and focus of Mary.

The challenge is to answer the call to a **"Martha Ministry"** while maintaining a **"Mary Heart"**.

It is awesome seeing Jesus being glorified in the everyday tasks of common chores and otherwise mundane activity. For years I have watched a young girl named Ruby, a Christian worker at a training center where we teach. I have consistently seen her alone sweeping floors, cleaning dishes, washing clothes, and working the garden, all while singing hymns and joyful songs. She'll offer me a cup of tea with a smile, and with the overflowing joy of sitting at the feet of Jesus she will attend to her chores and preparations. She works from before dawn until well after the evening meal.

As the ministry has grown, three other young ladies have joined her in the necessary labors: Helen, Lia, and Banisha. All of them now sing as they work, whether alone or together, they are working for the Lord Jesus in all that they do.

On a recent trip to that location we conducted a four-day training session for pastors in the area. "In the area" means anyone who can get to the training center with two days travel or less. So 45 local pastors were housed and fed for four days at the training center.

When it was over there was a great deal of work to do to clean up, bed sheets, blankets and other assorted laundry all needed to be washed. There are no washing machines or automated laundry facilities at that training center, so everything needed to be washed by hand. When I first heard the laughing and singing coming from the back of the house I thought someone was having a party. When I looked I saw Ruby leading her group of girls, Helen and Lia outside on a cloudy and chilly February day of 45 degrees. They were working through a mountain of laundry! It was a daunting task. But they were singing and laughing as they worked with cold water on a cold day to get everything clean. Ruby was putting the laundry in a big washbasin with soapy water and stomping around with her bare feet like she was crushing grapes, Helen was doing the same in her Washbasin to rinse the soap off, and Lia was wringing the laundry out and hanging everything on some temporary lines to dry in the sun. Banisha was inside cleaning the kitchen and cooking the meals for the day, and everyone was happy!

This scene went on ALL DAY, from early morning until the evening mealtime. I snuck outside to take a photo of the "Three Marthas" washing laundry and they caught me snapping a few pictures. That only made them laugh harder as they stomped around in their laundry washbasins. I realized that even though they were working hard with their hands, their hearts were sitting at the feet of Jesus. These young ladies have become like daughters to me. There is a joy within them that is just waiting to come spilling out at any moment. A Martha person with a Mary heart is a very valuable team member.

"Whatever you do, work heartily, as for the Lord, not for men...You are serving the Lord Christ."
(Colossians 3:23 ESV)

7) Peter the Point Man.

Peter was the apostle that was never afraid to speak up. He was undoubtedly the most visible and outspoken of the Twelve. He was never at a loss for words, and he was always ready to step up and speak his mind. After the resurrection of Jesus great understanding was given to Peter and he proclaimed the Gospel of Jesus boldly.

With a mission team there needs to be a "Point Man" to promote the trip. This often falls to Moses the Leader, but not always. If Moses tries to lead without someone to make the trip visible, no one will sign up to go and no funds will come in for the project.

How Peter the Point Man makes the trip visible and generates interest will depend largely on the purpose of the trip and culture of the church or organization. Bulletin announcements may be appropriate, and website information also works well. Some trips are too sensitive for public promotion because they travel into restrictive countries or hostile cultures. If that is coupled with a focus on specific training needs it may be necessary to make individual phone calls to qualified persons who would have the Martha skills and spiritual maturity together with the physical stamina for that particular trip.

Whatever the approach decided upon, Peter the Point man must make sure the word gets out. Peter is needed in order that people will sign up for the team, generate funds, and most importantly, pray for the team and the ministry objective.

"But Peter, standing with the eleven, lifted up his voice and addressed them: "Men of Judea and all who dwell in Jerusalem, let this be known to you, and give ear to my words." (Acts 2:14 ESV)

8) Ezra the Scribe.

Around 450 BC, Cyrus king of Persia made a proclamation that allowed the Jews to return to Jerusalem to rebuild the temple of the Lord. Ezra the scribe is the person who documented the process and made a record of all that took place. The result is the Book of Ezra in the Old Testament. Ezra prepared the way for Nehemiah and the complete rebuilding of Jerusalem including the wall.

On a mission trip there is a need to document what takes place. Our current day Ezra needs to be familiar with recording events in writing, but also visually in photos and videos. The position of Ezra on the team is extremely important in two specific areas.

1) As the team brings back the trip report to the church and supporters, Ezra is the key person to provide the needed information and documentation. This report to the church is discussed more fully in Chapter nine.

2) The other area of importance is the critical analysis of the trip. This analysis is done after the trip is completed. The information that Ezra documents is then used to critique different aspects of the trip so that good results can be expanded upon in the future, and less than favorable results can be used to address, change and re-focus ministry approaches. Since we are talking about long-term relationships and ongoing partnerships in ministry, each trip to a particular place is groundwork for the next trip to that location.

With each sequential trip, the ministry should become deeper, the relationships more mature and better prepared for the complete release of the ministry to the local church. Will there be plans for additional assistance to reach the next level and facilitate numerous other aspects of growth? The greatest growth of all is the relationships being built so these details can be discussed openly and honestly. Ezra is the key to these steps.

It was Ezra that helped us see that our approach to Children's ministry in Central America was not working. Our team was bringing a pre-packaged presentation that worked in North America to a culture, language and context where it did not fit. Ezra's photos and videos showed the disinterest of the children and the lack of connection with them. The team missed the problem in their excitement of making ministry happen. Ezra's work confirmed what our Central American partner said to me candidly during the skits. "This is not working!"

We salvaged the week by making some changes, but we completely changed our future approach to ministering to the children as a result of the failure that Ezra documented. For many years now the trips have been very productive as we devote our energies to helping our Central American partners become more successful in their ministry to their children. We no longer attempt to push our North American program on them. Great results! It is Ezra that also documents the successes and accomplishments of the team. Sometimes Ezra and Jethro are the same individual on the team, but they are distinct and perform two different roles.

As milestones are reached and ministry matures, it is Ezra that supplies the information and facts so that these successes can be reported back to the churches and built upon with proper initiatives in the future.

"And when they arrived and gathered the church together, they declared all that God had done with them, and how he had opened the door of faith to the Gentiles."
(Acts 14:27 ESV)

9) Timothy the Learner.

Timothy is Paul's son in the faith. The great apostle Paul poured his experience, wisdom, doctrine, insight and passion into Timothy. Timothy needs to be on your mission team. No matter where you go or how many times you go there, it is important to bring some people who need to learn. These could be first time team members or a veterans of short term mission trips, but there needs to be a desire within them to learn and grow into a life that includes service in missions. For Timothy this is not just an adventure into another culture where he is looking for an enhanced experience to feed his ego, put on a resume, or brag about to friends. Timothy realizes that the ultimate "enhanced experience" is becoming a true follower of Jesus. Second to that is helping others become true believers in Jesus. We do not want Timothy making all of the same dumb mistakes we made over the years (I know, they were "lessons" that taught us well!).

We need to train the next generation to continue fulfilling the commission of spreading the Gospel close to home and to the uttermost parts of the earth. The Timothy members of our trip need to shoulder some responsibility, step out in faith, experience success, accomplish something worthwhile, get frustrated when it is difficult, push through the problems, and follow up on next steps to be taken. They need some freedom to minister within their gifts, some flexibility to make their own mistakes, be challenged to step further out in faith, and have Paul (or Moses or David or Jethro) to look after them so they are in a safe place to grow.

> *"This charge I entrust to you, Timothy, my child, in accordance with the prophesies previously made about you, that by them you may wage the good warfare, holding faith and a good conscience."*
> *(1 Timothy1:18-19 ESV)*

10) Thomas the Norwegian, the OTHER disciple!

Thomas needs to be on your trip. He is not an Apostle, and he is not in the Bible, but he is a good Norwegian friend of mine! Tom stands about 6ft 5in tall and weighs about 300 lbs. He often sports a full beard. I usually introduce him as "Little Tommy". He just lumbers into the room or church service and makes his way to the front. People expect to see some little guy weighing 100 lbs., and they laugh when Tom walks in and bellows "You called?" Tom needs no translator, even though he speaks only English. His hearty laugh and lovable personality transcends language. It only takes a few minutes with Tom to feel at ease and comfortable. This is his God given gift. There is no hidden agenda, no manipulation, and no self-serving motivation.

Tom loves people and it is something that is impossible to hide. Tom can be the most important person on the trip. In a cross cultural situation, when awkward moments can become awkward hours, days and weeks, Tom is able to cut through the awkwardness and usher in an authentic, comfortable atmosphere.

WE NEED THOMAS! What does Tom do? We need to understand this because if there is not a natural Thomas on the trip, someone must fill this role. I have a few ideas on what Tom does;

- He authentically cares about the people he ministers to. That is something that cannot be faked. Tom has a real compassion for the people he meets and works with. It is evident in his attitude, conversation, behavior, and priorities. Thomas thoroughly enjoys being with the people. They become his friends.
- He is safe. Tom loves to laugh, but he never makes someone else the butt of the joke. If

anything—he makes fun of himself more than anything else. People know that Tom will never make them look bad. He is an encourager. People like to be around Tom.

- If there is something that needs to be said or someone needs correction, Tom will do that privately so as to not embarrass the person in public. If it must be in public, Tom will wrap the truth in Love and deliver the message with care and compassion.

- Tom is a team player. He wants the entire team of missionaries, local church members, pastors, indigenous leaders, and children to all be successful and encouraged. He is not the "everyone gets a trophy" type of guy; he actually wants to see each person experience authentic success. As a result people know that Tom is actually rooting for them, not just patronizing them. There is a BIG difference.

Well, sometimes Thomas is not there and the leader, Moses, needs to put some grease in the relational gears.

Many years ago I was in Cuba spending time with local leaders of the churches. It was a Sunday afternoon and we were just spending time together. Everyone spoke only Spanish except myself, and I spoke only English. My translator was called away for the afternoon and I was left to fend for myself. It was quickly awkward as we tried to communicate between long periods of silence. One of the Cuban pastors had a little daughter about three years old. She could not understand why I was speaking gibberish and she kept trying to get me to speak Spanish. I somehow communicated to them that I was studying Spanish but had not learned anything useful yet.

The Cubans began to poke fun at the little Spanish I spoke so poorly, and they asked me to share with them what I had learned. My recent Spanish classes were focused on animals, so I pointed to the biggest pastor in the room and asked, "¿Es esto un elefante? No, esto no es un elefante." Which means, "Is this an elephant? No, this is not an elephant." As I walked around the room pointing to different pastors and asking "¿Es este un tigre? No, esto no es un tigre." "Is this a tiger? No, this is not a tiger." And to another pastor I pointed and asked, "¿Es esta una tortuga verde? No esto no es una tortuga verde." "Is this a green turtle? No, this is not a green turtle." And I continued going around the room with all of the animals I had learned pointing to different pastors each time I asked the question. They began to laugh, and the laughing got more and more hilarious as I maintained a straight face while asking the questions.

At that point the little three-year old daughter came walking in after listening to the whole thing outside the room and she just stood there looking at me, so I asked her, "¿Soy un oso polar?" "Am I a polar bear?" She looked at me, laughed and said "Si! Un oso polar!" Yes, a polar bear! That just made everyone laugh harder, and they began to call me Pastor Oso Polar, which means Pastor Polar Bear! We all relaxed for the rest of the day and were comfortable with no awkwardness. We could still not communicate much, but just spending time together and walking around their town in a prayer walk was great. Many of those pastors have become key leaders and I still have good friendships with them. It all started with Thomas the Norwegian greasing the relational gears with some silly Spanish lesson.

One year later I visited the pastor who had the three-year old girl. She was then four years old, and when she saw me on the walkway she yelled "Oso Polar!" and ran to me to get a hug. To this day she and her family call me Pastor Oso Polar. Thomas the Norwegian is a very important member of the team.

"So if there is any encouragement in Christ, any comfort from love, any participation in the Spirit, any affection and sympathy, complete my joy by being of the same mind, having the same love, being in full accord and of one mind. Do nothing from selfish ambition or conceit, but in humility count others more significant than yourselves. Let each of you look not only to his own interests but also to the interests of others."
(*Philippians 2:1-4 ESV*)

****

Be aware of the different roles needed to be filled on your team, and remember to be flexible! You may need to assume several roles yourself and switch back and forth between them as the needs arise. Or you may need to ask someone to step up to the responsibility of one of these roles. Be cautious and prayerful who you choose. It is much easier to ask someone to step up than it is to ask him or her to step down.

126

Chapter Eight
The Personal Touch

The Money Question

I was cleaning off my desk (more like an archaeological dig) one morning when I came across a letter that I had forgotten about. I had planned to read it when I received it but had put it off for another time. Since I was trying to break that nagging and troublesome habit of procrastination, I sat down right then to read it. It was a letter from a dear friend who was preparing to go on a short-term mission trip to the Philippines.

The letter described the needs in that foreign land and the purpose of the trip in a manner that was factual and informative. Because of my close relationship with this friend I decided to respond to the request for financial support with a check for $25. Then I got to the bottom of the letter and realized that the trip had been over for a month! The letter had actually been sitting on my desk for more than four months. That's a little longer than I remembered!

I had missed the opportunity to be involved in my friend's trip and to bless him with prayer and financial support. What kind of friend was I to let this happen? And to make matters worse, I was a Missions Pastor! I am supposed to have a heart for missions and lost souls. I run my own short-term missions trips. And this was not the first support letter I had "misplaced".

It kept happening to me. I must be a failure!

The next day I was in my office at church where I served as an Associate Pastor in charge of missions, sulking and feeling like a failure, when I began to think through my pattern of reading mail and how I sort through it. I put junk mail in the garbage, and all impersonal newsletters, form letters, and bulk mailings get piled to the side where they sit until I have some time to read through them. Sometimes months go by before I get around to looking through this pile of mail that I classified as "impersonal and unimportant". This can lead to some embarrassing situations when some important things are missed.

One evening I vented with some friends about my problem of not reading and taking seriously these letters from those raising funds for mission trips. They admitted that they have the same problem! This happens to people all the time. We all have a tendency to rush through the mail and put the bills in one pile and the mail addressed to "Occupant", "Friend", "Neighbor", or "Valued Customer", in another pile to be sorted through and dealt with later. Letters addressed to us with our name neatly typed on the envelope, but inside it is typed "Dear _____" with our name hand written in the blank, we recognize as an impersonal form letter, and we often put it aside until later, even if it is from a close friend or relative.

Although we may have the best of intentions we often never see that letter again. I am not alone when it comes to falling short in responding to support letters. Great! However, I still didn't feel too good about it.

Several months later one of the college students from our Church who was attending an out of state Christian college stopped in to see me. Although I had seen him around church over the years when he was coming to Senior High youth group, we had never actually spoken. I was not even sure of his name. He was home for a break and wanted to know if the church could help pay for a missions trip he was planning to take in the spring. He handed me an envelope with no

128

name or address on it. The envelope contained a letter that began; "Dear _____." "Missions Committee at Northport" was written in the blank. The form letter that followed was well written; informative, factual, and explained well how I could send money. But it did not move me to take action. We had no previous relationship to act as a foundation to this request for funds. I was tempted to send him back to our youth pastor who undoubtedly knew him pretty well.

Instead I pointed to the letter he had handed me and asked if he had composed it himself and if there were other people he was giving it to? He told me that the professor teaching the missions course and organizing the trip had given everyone in the class a sample letter to follow. It had all the information on it and just needed to have the names filled in at the top. The students were then told to make a list of every person they knew. The list should include family, relatives, their friends, the friends and acquaintances of their parents, and **everyone** in their home church. If the church has a phone directory of its members, they were to use it as a mailing list. They should also send letters to other churches. The list needs to have at least 100 names. 200 would be better. The more letters sent out, the better chance they would have of getting a response and raising enough money for the trip.

As I sat listening to this young college student tell me of his fundraising plan I could not help but picture hundreds of his form letters being received in homes where they would be put aside with good intention but never responded to. If he had not handed the letter to me in person, I probably would never have read it. I told this young college student that I would speak to the other pastors about considering some financial support for him. As he left my office I thought, "There must be a better way."

We did decide to assist this young man with some funds, and over the next year I had the opportunity to speak with several other college students who were raising money for mission trips with their schools or a mission agency. Some of these large organizations send hundreds of students each year to places all over the world. The fundraising philosophy seems to be the same everywhere. Send lots and lots of form letters and hope to get a good return. Since only 10% of the letters are ever responded to, and since the usual support check is $25, a trip costing $1000 will require 400 letters to be sent. That is very hard or nearly impossible to accomplish, and most trips cost considerably more than that.

Given the cost of postage, team members would be starting their trip a few hundred dollars in the hole. Great pressure is then exerted on parents to pay up, and many of those raising money are told to ask their home church to make up the difference. Many smaller churches will not have the ability to pay for individuals to go on these short-term trips. In most churches the general budget is stretched to the limit already, and the mission budget is even tighter. Those professors teaching how to raise support seem to be missing the mark.

But where is the mark?

Some time later in the year I picked up my mail at the front desk and began walking down the hall to my office. I stopped in the middle of the hall and opened a letter and read it in its entirety while standing in the middle of the hall. It was a one-page letter from a fellow pastor thanking me for some help I had given him. The letter made me want to help him again in the future.

I continued to my office and sorted through the rest of my mail, putting impersonal mail in one pile to be looked at later, and the only personal piece of mail I received—the thank you letter from my pastor friend—I put in a special place. What was the difference between this letter and the other letters that caused two completely different reactions? For one letter I stopped everything and read the entire thing, the others I dropped in a pile headed for the trash. I then began to formulate a theory on how to use the dynamics of the letter that had stopped me in the hall. How do we reach people for the extremely important task of raising funds for mission trips. I had months to work on my theory before I had the chance to test it.

One afternoon a college student came to see me. She was the daughter of some very close friends. She had an idea for a mission trip that she wanted my advice on. It was a trip to experience missionary ministry within her area of study, and would be a great help to the missionaries she was planning to visit. The missionaries were well known to us and she was planning to go independently of any other group or mission board. Everything sounded great except she had no idea how to pay for the trip. It was an extended trip to Africa and was quite expensive. I decided to try out the theory I had been thinking and praying about.

The goal was to make sure that when a person received a letter from her, they would stop what they were doing, read it, and respond. So the experiment began.

These are the guidelines I gave her:

1. Pick 15 or 20 people to send letters to. They should be close friends and family, and are the people who are close enough to have dinner at your house. These are the people you have a close relationship with and care about you. This relationship is the foundation for this letter.

2. Design a letter that has three parts.
   a. **Greeting**. Each letter needs to start with a personal paragraph of greeting. (Hi Uncle Joe. How have you been? It was good to see you at Christmas time. Little Suzie is really getting big. Etc.) This paragraph must be authentic and real. It needs to emphasize the importance and depth of your relationship.
   b. **Body of the letter**. These are all the facts about the trip. **Who** you are helping, **what** you are doing, **where** you are going, **why** you feel God wants you to go, and **when** you are going.

      Include in this any needs you have or obstacles to overcome, such as passports, visas, relief supplies and necessary funds.
   c. **Response**. Give them two opportunities to respond to your need. Make it clear that they can be part of what God is doing, even though they will not be going with you themselves.
      * Ask for prayer. If you are serious about serving the Lord on this trip, you DO NOT want to go without prayer support.
      * Give them the information they need to send financial support.
3. All the letters you write can be identical except for the first paragraph. They should be one side of a full sheet of paper. After writing a personal greeting to the individual, the body of the letter and the response information is the same for each.

4. Include a self-addressed, stamped envelope with your letter.
5. Now this is the most important step of all. **Every letter must be hand written!** Address every envelope by hand. A personal hand written letter testifies of the importance of the relationship. It cuts through the impersonal medium of type and e-mail. It was the hand written envelope and thank you note that had stopped me in the hall months ago until I had read the whole thing. It stood out from everything else as **IMPORTANT**.

This college student was somewhat overwhelmed by the prospect of needing to write 20 letters by hand, but she agreed to give it a try. We agreed that all responses would be mailed to me at the church and all checks made out to the church. With each letter she would include an addressed and stamped envelope for the response.

As she left my office I could visualize people receiving letters from her. They would come home after a long day at work, grab the mail, flip through a bunch of bills, throw out the junk, put the stuff with pre printed labels on the side, and stop everything when they see their name written out by hand. They will open the letter and read the whole thing immediately, take out their checkbook and send in a nice contribution that very day. What a dream!

Of course I knew eventually my imagined result would be confronted by reality. Would my suggestion bear fruit or disappointment? What actually happened was this; within a week she had written 19 letters. Within three weeks I had received 18 responses. The smallest check was for $100; the largest was for $250. Her parents had not yet contributed, nor had the church. Her trip was completely paid for!

I figured maybe I had discovered something!

The next test came when I was preparing a team of 18 people to go to Cuba. I explained the entire "hand written" letter approach and they all agreed to try it. This time I had a mixed response. Some people received a lot of money quickly; others received little or none at all.

At one of our training meetings I repeated the guidelines. They all assured me they had followed them in every detail. So we waited. After weeks of no change we met again. Some people in the group had raised all the money they needed, some had raised MORE money than they needed, and some had nearly nothing. So I requested to see a sample of everyone's letter. They brought their letters to me and the results are as follows;

☐ Those 12 people who raised all their money and more had all followed the guidelines completely.

☐ Those 6 people who did not raise all their money had made some changes;

1. One person wrote a nice letter to each person, but did it on computer. The only hand written thing was the address on the envelope.
2. One person wrote beautiful letters to each person, but sent them all by E-Mail.
3. Two people sent impersonal form letters to everyone. (One was really bad!)
4. One person hand wrote some very personal but really bad letters.
5. And one person wrote all of her letters to her friends who were mostly college students who have no money to donate.

Regarding this last point, we must strike a balance in terms of who we ask to join our support team financially. I realize that a $15 donation from someone who can barely afford it can be as powerful as the widow's mite in scripture. I know one 10-year-old girl who has a real heart for the extremely poor students we work with in Nicaragua. She sets up a lemonade stand in front of her house and sells lemonade and cookies to raise money to help them. When she hands me an envelope full of coins and dollar bills, I know God is smiling. Her $32.65 donation is not a lot monetarily, but it sure is powerful. Having said that, you need to be alert to the fact that some people will not be able to support you financially, while others have the ability to fund your whole trip if they so desired.

Make sure you invite enough people onto your support team who are able to support you financially.

Since then I have tried this hand written approach many times with groups. I can almost always tell who wrote what kind of letter by the way the money comes in. Those who closely follow the guidelines almost always raise a lot of money. Those who ignore or change the guidelines almost always come up short on money. That is a great record.

This all makes sense when we think about God and His character. He is a personal God, He is our personal Savior, and He treats us as individuals. We become Christians one at a time. He answers our specific and individual prayers. We are used by Him in unique ways. Jesus called us "Friends". We are the "Bride" of Christ. We are His children. God did not call us to Himself with a form letter or a universal prayer; even the "Lords Prayer" in Scripture teaches HOW to pray in a personal way, it does not give us a formula of words to use. God called us to a relationship with Him through the shed blood of Jesus. God makes His written Word come alive to us uniquely as we read and search the Scriptures. He speaks to us individually even when we read the same Scripture collectively.

The salvation of a person is an extremely personal experience. There is nothing more intimate than an individual's faith, prayer life, and relationship with God. A mission trip, by its very nature, is a journey into the lives of people for the purpose of connecting them with—or inviting them to experience—a personal and intimate faith, prayer life and relationship with Jesus Christ. He is the personal, relational and loving Savior. Yet, we tend to approach fundraising for this intimate journey in the most impersonal, sterile, and business like manner possible. I believe that is wrong. I believe God wants to use our earthly relationships to build His Spiritual Kingdom. Financial relationships are not exempt from this dynamic.

We truly are the "Body of Christ". 1 Corinthians chapter 12 makes that point clear. The mission team functions as the "Hand" to reach into a foreign land with the Gospel of Jesus Christ. The Hand cannot do that alone; the whole body needs to be involved in that mission.

The process of writing support letters is much LESS about raising money than it is about mobilizing the Body of Christ into action to spread the Gospel. The letters we write must invite people to be part of the mission of crashing the gates of Hell. It is the process of developing a support team that is truly part of what you are doing as you follow the Lord in obedience.

Many people desire to be used by God in missionary work but are unable to go themselves. They need the opportunity to be part of what you are doing. This goes far beyond financial support. This is a dynamic that has its foundation built on a healthy relationship. **They can go on this mission trip THROUGH you,** prayerfully and financially. They must be invited to participate based on the relationship they have with you.

Having said that, do not rule out anyone who God brings into the support team. This includes unbelievers! God may be using the curiosity that unbelievers have about the trip to draw them into the family of believers. They will think it is strange that you give up your vacation and actually pay money to spend two weeks in a foreign land, sleeping on the floor and eating nothing but rice and beans. God is able to use the curiosity of unbelievers, along with their money, for His own purposes and glory. He may be using your trip to reveal Himself to them! When they look at you, they see God working.

"In the same way, let your light shine before others, so that they may see your good works and give glory to your Father who is in heaven."(Matthew 5:16 ESV)

That opens the door to the final step in the process, the personal report brought back to the supporters. We will talk more about bringing a report back to the church and those involved in your personal support team in the next chapter. Let us just say for now that when people realize that they have personally assisted in the changing of lives for eternity with the Gospel of Jesus Christ, they will look forward to the next trip you take and the opportunity to be part of that support team again.

My good friend, Thomas the Norwegian, who has accompanied me on many mission trips, has done an extremely good job of developing a healthy support team. When the announcement is made about an upcoming trip to Cuba, I receive support checks from people BEFORE Tom has a chance to write any letters! They are excited about how God uses Tom—and they want to be part of how God uses "The Other Disciple".

Principles do not change, but methods do change. **DO NOT** use the hand written letters as a formula or technique to bring in money. I have had a few people over the years that I barely know, listen to this teaching and send me hand written letters asking me for support. The letters were always personal and complimentary, but they were **FAKE**. There was no relationship to be personal about! They were trying to manipulate me by using my own teaching against me. It didn't work.

The efforts you make must be authentic and honest. If there is a way to connect with people in an authentic, relational way without hand writing letters, that is fine. The "Hand Written" aspect of the letter is simply the evidence of the personal relationship between you and the one receiving the letter. If you fake a personal relationship in an effort to pressure someone into giving, that will most likely backfire on you.

Be real. Be honest. Trust in God. Enjoy the adventure of fundraising—God uses this process for His honor and Glory.

139

Chapter Nine

The Return Policy

Non-Negotiable #5

In the mid 1990s I attended a Mission Conference at Regent University in Virginia Beach. There were two big name speakers that I wanted to hear from and I was excited to have the opportunity to hear them in person. I will not comment on their theology here, just on the approach each took to report to the church.

The first speaker was a very successful evangelist. He spent his entire time speaking about the tremendous successes of the crusades he was famous for in Africa. He was well known for having crusades throughout the continent that attracted many thousands of people. The evangelist described in detail how each night of the crusades he saw 20 thousand or more people come to faith in Christ because of his powerful preaching of the Gospel.

He was emotional and energetic, and the room was alive with excitement at hearing the great additions to the kingdom of God. But I found myself sinking deeper into my seat, becoming discouraged and hopeless. What was wrong with me? The rest of the room was energized, and I was depressed! I went back to my room that night and could not sleep. The pastor I was rooming with was energized and quoting the evangelist's sayings like "All switching is useless unless you are plugged in!" Great line, describing how you cannot turn on the power of the Holy Spirit unless you are plugged into God. But I just couldn't get excited. I laid awake most of the night feeling that I should just quit the ministry; after all, this evangelist was leading 20 thousand people to the Lord each day! I could easily count the number of converts I had made in my entire (short at that time) missions career! Why bother? This guy has this whole thing covered! Maybe I was not "plugged in!"

The next night was the second speaker I had wanted to hear. But at that point I did not want to go. I was discouraged enough already and did not need to get more depressed. I attended the meeting that night anyway. The second speaker was Brother Andrew. He was famous for smuggling Bibles into restricted countries and risking his life to get the Scriptures into the hands of those who had no access to the Gospel. As I listened to Brother Andrew speak I found myself sitting on the edge of my seat. The room was quiet as he spoke. There was not the excitement and energetic response from the audience as I had seen on the previous night. Some people even began to sneak out. They did not want to hear what Brother Andrew was sharing!

But I was riveted to my seat listening to every word Brother Andrew was saying. He spoke about the difficulties of ministry and the roadblocks to spreading the Gospel. I heard about the failures he experienced. He shared from his heart how the Lord encouraged him to continue in spite of the great sacrifices he and others were making to spread the Good News of Salvation. Brother Andrew was able to articulate the value of getting God's word into the hands of the lost, many of which were located in areas of the world where being a Christian could be punishable by death. He spoke about the ways he had seen God touch the lives of these precious people who were hungry for hope, and how the Lord worked around and through the police and military personnel who were supposed to stop and arrest those trafficking Bibles. Brother Andrew spoke about how each and every person was worth the risk they were taking, and how the Lord was being glorified and received into one heart at a time.

I went back to my room that night encouraged! This was real mission work! This was what I was called to do!

I lay awake that night wondering what the difference was between the famous evangelist and Brother Andrew. The first was like a pep rally that got people excited and pumped up. The second was serious and somber and some people walked away, not wanting to hear what was said about the difficulties and faith-stretching events in the mission field. But I was opposite! The pep rally discouraged me and the somber words of reality encouraged me!

Was I crazy?

As I lay awake I realized what was happening. I thought through the presentation of the evangelist and I realized that his entire talk was about the great accomplishments of the evangelist! He spoke about his awesome and talented preaching, his great crusades, his boldness to speak, his tireless schedule, and the amazing success of HIS efforts. There was little or no credit given to the Lord! It was all evangelist centered, not Jesus centered. And the evangelist took credit for the fruit of the successful crusades.

I asked myself **"How much of that fruit was "Fruit that lasts"?**

On the contrary as I thought through what Brother Andrew had spoken about, I heard about the great accomplishments of the Lord! All credit for every accomplishment, every border crossing, every bible delivered, and every soul touched was given to the Lord. Brother Andrew was more like a participating spectator watching the hand of God reach into difficult places and touch people one at a time. It was the Lord and His accomplishments that Brother Andrew spoke about, and he considered it a privilege to be a part of the plan of God to accomplish these things. It was personal!

This was real! This was the type of ministry I had experienced myself, with difficulties, hard work, one life at a time, and successes that can only be explained if the Lord is in charge. This was not over spiritualizing common events. This was real! Brother Andrew and I both had **"Fruit that lasts"**!

So what was the difference I saw in those two conference reports?

The famous evangelist was the focus of his own report while Brother Andrew made God the focus of his report. (I am commenting only on the presentations and reports given at the conference, I am not commenting on their theology or approach to ministry and techniques.)

It was then that I purposed myself to be a Brother Andrew type of speaker when I report back to the church on what was happening in the mission field. Yes, there are things **WE** work at to advance the Kingdom of God, but God **must** get the credit for that. It is important to report to people exactly what we did when we were in the mission field, but when we report what **WE** did we must also report what the **LORD** did.

This speaks more about the attitude we have when we return, not about the list of accomplishments. Sadly, most of the reports from teams returning from short-term trips resemble the famous evangelist's report, not the Brother Andrew report. We hear all about the TEAM accomplishments, not the accomplishments of the Lord. The team tells how the project couldn't have been completed without them showing up and taking control, or how the local people had never had a team as awesome and wonderful as

144

them, or how they solved a multitude of problems, or how 12 high school girls on the team built two houses for the poor people, and so on. The focus of the report is most often completely on the awesomeness of the team.

Once in a while we hear from a team that has a Brother Andrew heart. We hear about a project that the local people were struggling with and how the Lord prepared the team to partner with them and assist them to become successful in completing their own project. Then the local people asked about this "Jesus" the team was talking about. He must be real because they felt genuine concern and care from team members, not pity or a superior attitude. And the team shared real solutions to the real problems they encountered, helping the local people to solve their own issues in a Biblical way. And they assisted two men in building houses for their families. The local men shared their building techniques, tools and know-how with the team. There are reasons for the way they build in that environment and culture, and these people in this remote place are actually more talented builders than we are! The team learned valuable lessons, built friendships and trust in an authentic way.

Both teams accomplished similar things, but one team was focused on the awesomeness of their own group, the other team had a heart focus on the awesomeness of God. There are a few verses in the Bible that speak about the correct attitude we should have as Christians, and especially as we move across cultures to share the Gospel.

The Bible speaks about believers being the light of the world. We looked at part of this verse in the last chapter to keep our fundraising focus on the Lord. It is equally important here.

"You are the light of the world. A city set on a hill cannot be hidden. Nor do people light a lamp and put it under a basket, but on a stand, and it gives light to all in the house. In the same way, let your light shine before others, so that they may see your good works and give glory to your Father who is in heaven."
(Matthew 5:14-16 ESV)

The light is not there for its own benefit; it is there to illuminate that which a person needs to see. You are the light of the world. Your purpose is NOT to bring attention to yourself, but to illuminate your Father in Heaven so that others will be drawn to Him, not drawn to you. The Bible talks about this.

"Do nothing from selfish ambition or conceit, but in humility count others more significant than yourselves. Let each of you look not only to his own interests, but also to the interests of others." (Philippians 2:3-4 ESV)

Unfortunately, many teams are only focused on the interests of the team and their own personal ambitions. They consider themselves superior to and better than those they go to serve. As a result, most reports given to churches from returning teams give the impression that the light the team was shining was illuminating the team itself, not the Father! The team itself is presented as being far above and superior to the people they went to help.

Luke 10:1-20 tells us that it was after some intense teaching that Jesus appointed seventy-two of His followers to go out and proclaim that the "Kingdom of God is near." The urgency of the task is evident by the instruction not to greet anyone on the road. This was not a command to be unfriendly, but a command that underscores the importance of the mission they were about to embark on. There are instructions on how to enter towns and homes, what to take, how to act, who to speak to, and so on. There are even instructions on how to leave when people will not listen.

Then there is a warning of destruction given in verse 12 on what will happen to those who will not listen to the message. This warning is given to the seventy-two being sent—so that they will understand more fully the great importance of the mission they were sent on. Also, notice the spirit of humility given to the seventy-two in the instructions.

The seventy-two returned from their mission with joy. They returned to Jesus and the other followers with great encouragement about how they had been **used by God** throughout their journey. The focus was on how they were used by God, not their own accomplishments. It is certain they told others how God had used them. They themselves were in the stories they told. But the reports were not about their own greatness. The reports all centered on what God had done. Since they were the ones experiencing and involved in the works God was doing, it was not possible to relate the stories without including themselves, but the main character and the source of their encouragement was God alone!

The vision of a worldwide Church containing believers from every tribe and nation is something that most Christians in North America will never see first hand. When the short-term team returns home they will serve as ambassadors, the eyes and ears of the congregation to see the world from God's point of view. Giving a report to the church with a "Brother Andrew" heart is not so easy, it goes against human nature. But if the team begins with the end in mind, wanting to bring a God glorifying report back to the church after the trip is completed, it will help everyone to stay focused on the Lord, not the team.

If this book has been helpful, the attitude of Brother Andrew will be evident when a report is brought back to the church. The final Non-Negotiable:

Non-Negotiable #5:
Bring the Blessing Back to the Church

When your trip is complete and everyone is home safe—your job is not over! Now is the time to return to your home church and body of believers with reports of how God has revealed Himself on this journey of yours. Bring the blessing back to those who have sent you.

This is extremely important.

Those who have sponsored you financially need to know they were a part of the work of God on your trip. If they know you were a good investment, they will be willing to invest again. Send them a personal letter and a photo or two as a personal report. Some of your supporters will not be part of your church and that letter you send after the trip will be the only report they receive.

If any non-believers sponsored you (as we discussed in the last chapter about raising funds) this report back to them is POWERFUL! Don't miss the opportunity!

Possibly you will get some time to report to the church on a Sunday morning. This is great, and also difficult. Be cautious on who shares what. If every team member shares, many of them may just say the same thing over and over. Assign them a subject and give them ONE MINUTE each! (They'll take two) Or, use a person who can communicate well and understands the importance of the things shared in this chapter.

Give God the glory in an authentic way.

It is tempting to begin with the focus on God and then turn the spotlight back on the team. For example, "God showed up on this trip and used the awesome talent of each person on the team, and here is how..." and then go on to give glory and accolades to the team, leaving God out of the picture altogether.

Sometimes you will only get the opportunity to share on a personal level, possibly one on one, or in a small group or Bible study. Prepare for that. Prepare a 30 second response for the person who asks you about the trip on Sunday morning while passing in the church lobby, or on the checkout line at the grocery store. Then have a 5–10 minute response for someone who has a little more time, or if your small group gives you a few minutes to share. And finally, have a longer and more complete report to give to those who are really interested, or if your small group gives you the entire meeting to share. These smaller sharing times can be more effective than the whole church report so do not neglect them.

If we again use the **"body"** analogy that the apostle Paul uses in 1 Corinthians 12, and we touched on in previous chapters, we can liken the mission team to the hand that is sent into a foreign land to accomplish a particular task. The hand is connected to the arm, and the arm is connected to the rest of the body. The hand cannot accomplish this task without the support and strength of the body. The body is willing to send the hand out to accomplish more tasks, but the eye needs to see results before the body is willing to support another extension of the hand to accomplish another task.

As you return to your home church and community, your job is to bring the results of your mission trip back to the body of Christ.

This is the ultimate "Return Policy."

Chapter Ten
Face-to-Face

Pastor Alex is a pastor in Nicaragua. He pastors in a poor town just outside the capitol city of Managua. I got to know Pastor Alex quite a few years ago when I became involved in the training of pastors there. One year we were working with some of his ministry leaders at his church and I commented on how nice his church building was. For this small poor town the church building was really very nice. It was probably the nicest building in town. He began to tell me the story of how the church and building had come to be.

On that site had been a private house that was the center for prostitution, drugs, and all sorts of other activities that plagued the neighborhood. He and others in the church tried for years to reach the owners of the house with the Gospel, but there was no progress and things just got worse. So the church went to prayer. They prayed that the Lord would remove this problem from the community and restore safety to the neighborhood.

Shortly after the church began to pray, the family living in the house offered it for sale! The church members wasted no time in raising the funds to purchase the dilapidated house. Some of the members gave funds with great sacrifice to accomplish the purchase. The house was acquired and immediately knocked to the ground to ensure that there would be no more disturbing activities taking place there. The neighborhood immediately celebrated a newfound safety and security. Soon the church decided to complete the testimony of the goodness of God and use the previously defiled property to build a new church building and move out of their cramped facility.

Money was raised again and the construction began. Men from the church and community gave of their time when they were able, and as the weeks went by the cement block walls grew higher and higher. There was great excitement as the new building took shape, and they hoped to be in the new church within a year. But as the funds began to slow down, the excitement waned and so did the work. People in the congregation got busy with their own lives and the progress on the building stopped. The walls were complete, but there was no roof. At this point they had moved out of their old building and were meeting in the new building and it was wide open to the sky! Pastor Alex told me that during the rainy season they all prayed and the rain always seemed to stop when it was time for service!

Pastor Alex paused his story at this point and invited me to his home where we could sit and continue our conversation in a quiet place. We walked around the back of his church and around an old tool shed. He stopped at the door and walked into the shed. This was no tool shed—this was his home! It was a small, one room place with two old chairs on the one side of the room. There was a small kitchen area, and no bathroom! They used the bathroom in the church when they needed it! He continued his story as we sat together.

They met in the church with no roof for many months and there was not enough money to finish the project. They were stuck. Months went by with no progress. Then one day when Pastor Alex was in the shower (in the church bathroom), he felt God was speaking to him, "Sell your motorcycle and give the money to the church for the roof." At first he thought he was crazy for thinking that. The small motorcycle was the only transportation his family had. But he could not shake the feeling that God was asking him to sell the motorcycle and give the money for the church roof. So he made a deal with God. He said to God that if his wife agreed to sell the motorcycle and give the money to the church for the roof, he would do it! He thought that was pretty safe; his wife would never agree to sell the only transportation the family had. So after his shower he went home and asked his wife what she thought about the idea of selling the motorcycle and giving the money for the roof.

Well, she thought it was a great idea! Oh no! Now he was stuck. He couldn't fight God AND his wife! So he cleaned up the motorcycle and sold it. He then gave the money to the church for the roof—without saying anything to the church members. Soon people saw that he was walking a lot and there was no motorcycle. Someone found out and leaked the fact that Pastor Alex had sold his only mode of transportation and had given the money to the church for the roof. Soon people began to give to the roof project. If their pastor was going to sell his motorcycle for the benefit of the church, they would sell their things also! Some people sold their TV sets and DVRs so they could contribute. Then they had a garage sale at the church and people donated some of the nicest things they owned to raise money for the roof. Many gave again at great sacrifice to themselves.

Some of the other local churches found out about what was going on and joined in to help with the cost of the project and the labor to finish it. Eight weeks later it was complete! All because an obedient pastor followed the leading of God and stepped out in faith and humility. Today the old house of prostitution and drugs is gone and a faith based church stands in its place, testifying to the God of redemption and provision.

I sat in that humble little home I had mistaken for a tool shed and listened to that remarkable journey of faith. I could not help but think that I was sitting in a home that contained more riches than most homes back in North America. The strong faith and dependence on God were inspiring. My mind drifted to some of the individuals I knew back home that had big bank accounts and owned multiple cars, boats, big houses, vacation homes, and so much more, but were living in spiritual poverty. The things they thought they owned—actually owned them! They spent their time caring for their cars, boats, and other possessions that will one day rust away in a junkyard or be buried in a landfill. At the same time they were neglecting the only things that really last: their faith, their family and their relationships. Their possessions had become their gods and there was no room for Jesus. They were certainly not going to sell their hard earned possessions and give the money away! I am sure we all know people like this. Some of us WERE those people before Jesus got hold of our hearts, and some of us reading this last chapter still ARE those people. Sadly some of us keep slipping back to where we came from.

Sometimes we travel to the mission field on a short term trip with the great expectation of being used by God to reach the lost, spread the Gospel, encourage the believers and missionaries, accomplish a needed task and give of ourselves. We can go with pure hearts and great motives, make all the right decisions and be thoroughly prepared. Then we run smack into someone like Pastor Alex and we realize that sometimes the people we are attempting to help—are actually helping us! We see actions that are rooted in deep faith, attitudes that reflect a dependence on God for everything, and a humility that recognizes the absolute sovereignty of the Lord. We in North America have money, education, opportunity, and a lot of material goods, but when we encounter real Christians with real faith and a real dependence on God, we realize how poor we really are—without Christ.

We started this book with a chapter on Stone Movers. Jesus was about to perform a great miracle and raise Lazarus from the dead. But Jesus stood in front of the tomb and asked someone to "Move the Stone." There was a huge stone standing between Jesus and Lazarus. Jesus wanted nothing to block the way between him and the one he loved. After the stone was moved, Jesus called Lazarus and removed death from him.

Sometimes I think that when we travel to the mission field on a short-term trip, Jesus asks some of the people we meet to "Move the Stone" for US—so WE can see Jesus. Even as Christians that stone sometimes rolls back to the place where it once blocked us from seeing and hearing Jesus clearly. The stone that blocks us from Jesus can be many things: money, possessions, cars, boats, and houses. Or it can be our job, our position, our hobby, our children or our spouse. Anything can become a stone that blocks us from Jesus, even our church! Some of the most resilient stones that are hardest to move are rooted in pride. Pride puffs us up and sneaks into our life undetected, or masquerading as humility. We want to feel good about ourselves so we help others out of guilt. We want others to respect and like us, so we try to earn their approval. But when we take a short-term trip and someone dares to roll away the stone that has been blocking us from Jesus, we suddenly come face to face with real faith. It is both humbling and inspiring to witness authentic faith in difficult circumstances.

Jesus is still doing miracles and sometimes that miracle happens when He reaches into our heart to reveal Himself to us more fully. Pastor Alex moved a stone in my life when he shared the story about his church building, roof and motorcycle. Sometimes the person who moves the stone in our life is one that we least expect!

Let me tell you about Reyna.

We began a scholarship program in Nicaragua to help students go to High School. In many of the poor communities the students attend school until grade 6 at a local neighborhood elementary school, and then quit. Grade 7 begins High School and goes for five years until grade 11, and it is free. However there is a problem; the school could be 5 or 10 miles away. How do they get there? The bus and other expenses are $25 per month, and some families have a monthly income of $40 or so. High School is not a possibility for those students.

At 14 years of age the boys join a gang, and the girls are often told by their mothers to go out and find a man to move in with and get him to take care of them. When the girls become pregnant the man they live with often throws them out, and they move back with mom in a situation worse than the first. The cycle of poverty and lack of education repeats itself again and again.

With the oversight of a school principal and the partnership of a local ministry the "Bus Scholarship" was formed. We started with ten students. Reyna was one of these first ten students beginning seventh grade in High School. She was an awkward, shy 13 year old who was very excited about the adventure of continuing her education. I immediately liked Reyna, but she was afraid to speak with me. I was a scary foreigner! So I just kept an eye on her and prayed for her. My wife and I decided to personally sponsor her scholarship.

A year later we added ten more students to the program. A year after that we added another ten. In the third year of the scholarship program we were together with the students during a 3-day retreat, and our organization was making up a brochure about the scholarship so we could promote some sponsorships. I watched while photos were taken of each student. Some people just look amazing in photos. No matter what the light or surroundings, they just look awesome. Some of these Nicaraguan students looked so good that I was not sure we could raise funds using these photos! Perfect skin tone, perfect smile, perfect photos. Reyna was NOT one of those people! Every photo just looked terrible! We tried everything and finally picked the least bad photo. I could see Reyna was discouraged. The next day I took my translator over to speak with Reyna, and after a little conversation I touched her on the shoulder and told her that my wife and I were the ones sponsoring her scholarship, and that I had been watching her for the past few years. I was impressed with her schoolwork, high grades and hard work, and I thought she was a special girl. I then asked her if there were any problems or situations in her life that I could pray for. She just looked at me, started crying and ran away. I looked at my Nicaraguan translator and asked if I had done something wrong? She was just as surprised as I was at Reyna's reaction.

The next day as the retreat was ending, Reyna came to me a little teary and apologized for her reaction to my questions. She did not know how to respond to my request to pray for her. She told me "No one ever cared about me and no one ever prayed for me before. I didn't know how to answer you." Then Reyna asked me to pray for her success in school and for her home life. She jumped on the bus and was gone. Well, I thought, "This is a special girl, I will certainly pray for her." I also spoke to the principal who was overseeing the scholarship program and had become a good friend of mine over the years. I asked her for some more information on Reyna and her family.

It took a few years to get a complete picture of Reyna's situation and to build a good relationship with her. Her story is not uncommon in Nicaragua. Her father deserted the family and left her mom with the kids. When Reyna was 8 years old her mom re-married and Reyna's stepfather had a violent temper. He would supply food for Reyna and her sisters, but no uniforms for school or other necessities. He would say, "You are not my children!" There was no telling when his terrible temper would erupt. He refused to let Reyna's mom work outside the home, but sometimes she would sneak some laundry work for the neighbors to earn a little money.

When Reyna's two older sisters each turned 14 years old, their mother made them leave the house to find a man to care for them. They never returned to live in the home. When Reyna turned 14 years old her mother told her the same thing—to leave the house and do whatever it takes to find a man to care for her. She was no longer welcome to stay in the home. Reyna refused! She said, "I am in Pastor Paul's scholarship program and I am going to go to High School!" So Reyna stayed home and continued to go to school. But it was not easy. Her stepfather was abusive and stopped supplying food for her. Her older sisters ridiculed her and attacked her for her moral purity and staying in school. This continued through the five years of High School. Reyna worked a job as a housekeeper to earn some money to live on. As I got to know Reyna better she became more open with me and my wife, Karen. When Reyna graduated High School I made a big deal about it. I told her how proud I was of her. She started crying again and told me "No one has ever been proud of me before." Then she said, "You are the father I never had." Reyna began to call me "Dad."

Because Reyna was an excellent student with very high grades, she qualified for University! So we kept her in the scholarship program and she began a five-year program focused on the Import/Export industry and international customs. But her home life was becoming worse. Her stepfather resented her and her mom constantly pushed her to leave the home.

However, Reyna realized she was the stabilizing factor in the home and she had three younger siblings she was concerned about, so she continued to live in the home. But she did have a secret dream. Her dream was to live at Villa Esperanza. Villa Esperanza (The Village of Hope) is a beautiful place where girls who have been abused—or are at risk of being abused—are given a nice place to live that is safe, clean and healthy. The scholarship student retreats each year were held at the Villa, and the directors are good friends of mine. They are also partners in overseeing the Bus Scholarship program. Reyna was very familiar with Villa Esperanza and dreamed of living there so she could finish her university studies in peace and safety. However, Villa Esperanza was full to capacity and had a waiting list. Reyna just kept her dream tucked away.

Time went by and two years into her University studies, the situation at home became so bad for Reyna that her mother threw her out of the house to appease the stepdad. Reyna had no place to live, and stayed with a friend for a few days. Reyna sent me an email asking me to pray for wisdom for her, and guidance from Jesus to make good decisions. Well, I contacted my good friends at Villa Esperanza and asked them to please find a spot and interview Reyna as a possible candidate to live at the Villa. This seemed like an emergency situation and a perfect solution. I was willing to cover all costs and support for Reyna so the Villa would not be burdened. They agreed and began the interview process with Reyna.

The thought that her dream to live at the Villa might just come true was exciting to Reyna. Living at the Villa would give her the opportunity to concentrate on the few remaining years at University while living in a safe, healthy place, with good food and a Christ centered environment.

The directors soon informed Reyna that she was accepted to live at the Villa! Her dream had come true! Reyna's life was about to take a turn for the better. No more abuse from the stepdad, no more problems, no more attacks from older sisters, just peace and serenity. So I was quite shocked when Reyna told me that she was going to TURN DOWN the opportunity to live at the Villa! I had gone to a lot of trouble for her and was adjusting my finances to cover the expense of fulfilling her dream and she was TURNING IT DOWN!

Then the Stone Moved.

Reyna knew that the hope existing in the lives of her younger siblings was only possible because she was the stabilizing force in the home. The safety of her mom depended on Reyna's presence in the home, and the people she loved were much more important to her than her own comfort and the dream of living at the Villa. Her desire for the love of Christ to fill and consume her family was much more powerful than her dream of living at the Villa. After much prayer and seeking the Lord the situation at home changed enough for Reyna to return to the house and she reestablished herself there. She continued to bless her Mom and honor her stepfather while being the beacon of light in the home. Reyna willingly accepted the responsibilities that she saw as her load to carry. She then placed her Burden in the hands of her Lord. Reyna wrote this to me in an email just after turning down the opportunity to live at the Villa:

"When I think of what God has done with me and how He moves my heart, I cry tears of joy because truly the love of God is perfect and HE is perfect."

Truly Reyna is a special girl. The love of Christ is in her and upon her. She has grown from an awkward seventh grade student to an absolutely beautiful, accomplished, Spirit filled university graduate. The most beautiful thing about Reyna is her heart—filled with Jesus. My life has been impacted by the faith and perseverance I see in Reyna. Her actions have Moved another Stone in my life and I have come face to face with real authentic faith in Jesus Christ.

While writing this final chapter I received a letter from Reyna. Please allow me to share a portion of it here. It gives further testimony to authentic faith.

"I have experienced that life is not easy if you do not go hand in hand with Jesus and that is why I am afraid to get away from Him because my life depends on Him only. Because everything that I have achieved and everything I have had for my life, my health, my family, everything has been from Him. Although sometimes I do not understand some things that happen in all my life. I have had problems with my sisters. My problems and my struggles are made with those that I love most and it hurts me to realize these things. You know my story and you know I fear God. My heart wants to honor God and honor my mother and make a difference, to break these chains and curses. Thank God my younger sisters are dedicating themselves to their studies with great effort. With the help of God and you Dad, I have achieved many things that none of my older sisters could achieve."

If our focus on mission work is mostly humanitarian, we will miss a great opportunity. We can build hospitals, set up feeding programs, establish scholarships, dig wells, paint fences, build schools, facilitate disaster relief, and give houses to the homeless. But if we do that without connecting the people to Jesus, what have we done? When the people we have helped in purely humanitarian ways die without Jesus:

They go to Hell healthy, wealthy and smart!
We have done nothing!

Reyna has embraced the Lord Jesus. She is an extremely rich girl. Her education, her health, and her future success are all just fringe benefits to the true riches within her heart. And Pastor Alex is spreading his immense wealth throughout his community. These are the immeasurable riches of a relationship with Jesus.

I trust as you participate in mission work you will be challenged and encouraged by what you experience. I pray you will have the opportunity to Move Stones for those who need to have a clear and unobstructed view of Jesus, and I pray that you don't miss those opportunities when they come your way disguised as problems. I hope the Lord arranges for you to meet authentic people of faith like Pastor Alex and Reyna who will Move some Stones in your life and impact your heart so you see Jesus clearer.

Expect to see miracles that glorify Jesus.

Expect to see people come face to face
with the Living Savior.

Expect to come face to face with Jesus yourself—when
you least expect it!

The Stone that Moves may be your own!

Appendix

Stone Movers   John 11 *(Chapter One)*

The Physically Dead
1. Lazarus was physically dead. He could not move the stone or help himself in any way.

2. The followers of Jesus COULD Move the Stone. Their obedience to Move the Stone was the ONLY thing they could do.

3. Jesus made a choice to involve His followers in this great miracle and victory over death. Jesus waited until the stone was moved before He called the dead to life.

4. Lazarus had the responsibility to respond to the call of Jesus. No one could respond for Lazarus, and no one could do the miracle except Jesus.

The Spiritually Dead
1. Without Jesus, people are spiritually dead and hopelessly lost. They cannot help themselves in any way.

2. The followers of Jesus CAN be obedient and Move the Stone that is blocking the clear path to Jesus and His promise of eternal life.

3. Jesus chooses to use His followers to preach the Gospel and testify to the world about Him. Jesus includes His followers in His victory over Satan.

4. The Lost and spiritually dead are responsible to respond to the call of Jesus. No one can respond for them. No one can grant eternal life to them— except Jesus

The Load and the Burden
(Chapter Two)
Galatians 6

1. The "**load**" consists of the normal, every day cares that each of us must bear to get through life. It is necessary for each man to shoulder the responsibility of his own upkeep.

2. The "**burden**" includes an excess amount of life's troubles that must be shared from time to time. When situations arise that are over and above the normal "load" that each person is expected to carry through life, the burden is to be shared by others.

Five types of trips
(Chapter Three)

1. Survey

2. Experiential

3. Physical

4. Teaching & Training

5. In the Trenches

Four Things to Look for Before a Trip
(Chapter Three)

1. Doctrine

2. Biblical Authority Structure

3. Successes

4. Problems

The Five Non-Negotiable of Short-Term Mission trips

1. There must be a reason to go.
   (Chapter Three)

2. Be a blessing and not a burden.
   (Chapter Four)

3. There must be connection with local people.
   (Chapter Five)

4. The team must minister to itself.
   (Chapter Six)

5. Bring the blessing back to the church.
   (Chapter Nine)

The Disciples on Your Trip
(Chapter Seven)

Moses the Leader	Authority figure/decision maker
David the Shepherd	Cares for the sheep
Paul the Apostle	Able to preach a message
Joshua the Strategist	Keeps the team focused
Jethro the Observer	Observes, watches, & advises
Martha the Worker	Has the skill for the task
Peter the Point Man	Makes the trip visible
Ezra the Scribe	Records the trip
Timothy the Learner	One(s) who needs to learn
Norwegian Thomas	Greases the relationship gears

Three points of a personal testimony
(Chapter Seven, Paul)

1. Your life before Christ

2. How you met Christ

3. Your life after Christ

Made in the USA
Middletown, DE
02 December 2019

79820362R00095